Cosimo De' Medici - Primary Source Edition

Katharine Dorothea Ewart, Katharine Dorothea Vernon

Nabu Public Domain Reprints:

You are holding a reproduction of an original work published before 1923 that is in the public domain in the United States of America, and possibly other countries. You may freely copy and distribute this work as no entity (individual or corporate) has a copyright on the body of the work. This book may contain prior copyright references, and library stamps (as most of these works were scanned from library copies). These have been scanned and retained as part of the historical artifact.

This book may have occasional imperfections such as missing or blurred pages, poor pictures, errant marks, etc. that were either part of the original artifact, or were introduced by the scanning process. We believe this work is culturally important, and despite the imperfections, have elected to bring it back into print as part of our continuing commitment to the preservation of printed works worldwide. We appreciate your understanding of the imperfections in the preservation process, and hope you enjoy this valuable book.

Foreign Statesmen

COSIMO DE' MEDICI

1389-1464

COSIMO DE' MEDICI

BY

K. DOROTHEA EWART
LATE SCHOLAR OF SOMERVILLE COLLEGE, OXFORD

London
MACMILLAN AND CO., Limited
NEW YORK: THE MACMILLAN COMPANY
1899

All rights reserved

Ital. 3346.2

Sumner fund

I WISH to express my sincere thanks to Mr. Armstrong, of Queen's College, Oxford, for his kind help, both in suggestion and criticism, and in the revision of the proofs.

K. D. E.

CONTENTS

CHAPTER I

INTRODUCTION—FLORENCE UNDER THE OLIGARCHY . . . 1

CHAPTER II

THE BANISHMENT AND RESTORATION OF COSIMO DE' MEDICI 41

CHAPTER III

FOREIGN POLICY FROM 1435 TO 1447—THE VENETIAN ALLIANCE—THE BALANCE OF POWER . . . 73

CHAPTER IV

FOREIGN POLICY FROM 1447 TO 1464—THE CONQUEST OF MILAN FOR SFORZA—THE FRENCH AND MILANESE ALLIANCES 105

CHAPTER V

THE DOMESTIC POLICY OF COSIMO DE' MEDICI AND THE CONSOLIDATION OF HIS POWER 140

CHAPTER VI

Character and Bases of Cosimo's Rule—His Private Life 183

CHAPTER VII

Cosimo's Patronage of Literature and Art . . 209

APPENDIX

List of Principal Authorities 239

CHAPTER I

INTRODUCTION—FLORENCE UNDER THE OLIGARCHY

WE, who live in the nineteenth century, are accustomed to the life of a vast state with a population of many millions, to foreign relations which concern the destinies of the whole world, and to domestic affairs, in which the few politicians who appear on the stage of action are merely representative of the interests of large classes and parties. For us, therefore, it is difficult to recognise Cosimo de' Medici as a statesman who required little less tenacity of purpose than a Bismarck, little less diplomatic skill than a Richelieu. For it may seem to us no great achievement for a man to make himself master of a little city-state, with a few thousand inhabitants, and a territory about as large as Yorkshire, and to carry on a career of successful diplomacy amongst other states of the same size, and extending but seldom beyond Italy. Yet, since to the student of political science and of statecraft the Florence of the fifteenth century and the Medicean power in Florence present political phenomena distinct from, though always related to, those appearing in any other state or period, the life of Cosimo de' Medici is worth studying, not only from the romantic point of view, as that of a man with a remarkable character and extraordinary career, but as a chapter in the History of Politics, with a significance and an interpretation of its own.

And first it should be realised that Florence, though a city, was a state, and as such totally distinct from the Florence of to-day, or from the English towns with which we are familiar. In her were to be found almost all the elements of national, as well as of municipal, life. She was far more independent, far more truly national, than the mediæval German free towns; the only parallel that can be in any way applied to her is that of the Greek cities, with whose life Aristotle has made us familiar. And Florence was more than a state, she was even in miniature an empire, since she ruled over several subject towns, each with its own measure of autonomy in domestic affairs, but all subject to the Imperial authority of the head city. Thus with Florence and her Tuscan Empire can best be compared Athens and her Empire about the shores of the Aegean Sea; and the comparison may be pursued yet further, and the rule of Cosimo over Florence compared with that of Pericles over Athens. The parallel can only be rough and superficial, yet we may remember that each founded his power upon the "people," as opposed to the "aristocracy"; that each first rose to supremacy upon the abortive attempts of his enemies to ostracise him, resulting in the exile of the enemies themselves; that each counted on preserving his power by leading the state to embrace a new line of foreign policy; that each was ruler of his state at the time of the two greatest outbursts which the world has ever seen of the spirit of man into fresh regions of art and thought.

And not only was Florence a state, she was also a modern state, in many respects one of the first of modern states. As her painters and savants stood at the head of the Renascence as the earliest artists and thinkers of the modern world, so her politics were now emerging from mediævalism and taking a modern complexion. England, in the first half of the fifteenth century, had barely begun to emerge from the Middle Ages. There were to be found in her the hasty recourse to brute force in all matters of dispute, the dominating influence of the Church, the wide scope of the feudal idea as the chief characteristics of history; the possession of land was still the one mark of social status, political theory and diplomacy were yet in their infancy. But the Italy of this date was the Europe of the sixteenth or seventeenth centuries in miniature. The political conditions in which Cosimo had to work were largely those of modern, not of mediæval politics. War was now "waged chiefly by reputation," the Church as a Church had no political influence,—for the position of the Pope was hardly distinguished from that of the head of a secular state; feudalism had ceased to be a force in politics. Political theory was discussed even in the market-place; Cosimo himself contributed to what had already been acquired the theory of the Balance of Power among states, and, with some help from Francesco Sforza, invented and elaborated those methods of diplomatic intrigue by which the balance of power was maintained, and which were to last as long as it lasted.

Florence, too, was a commercial state; the possession of land was merely an accident in the possession of power,—a part, but the least important part, of wealth; we find all the commercial problems of a later date already alive,—the uneasy relations between capital and labour, the employment of foreign politics as a means to commercial extension, the manipulation of a state debt, with shares whose value fluctuated as the prosperity of the Government.

Here, too, are found in almost every individual that very modern craving to obtain a share, however small, in the direction of the national policy; here, as in modern politics, the difficulty of establishing an executive powerful enough and sufficiently many-sided to embrace and cope with the complicated and manifold conditions of modern administration; here efforts like those of a modern foreign minister to make his policy consistent and effective, and yet agreeable to the public whim. Government must be maintained either by brute force or by clearly-expressed public opinion, never by the inert acquiescence of the governed in any rule that had an appearance of hereditary right.

Yet the size of the Italian, like that of the Aristotelian, city-state could not but introduce many conditions which differentiate it from modern nations. To take part in politics was the privilege of a very limited class of fully-enfranchised citizens of the town; the poor, the country people, and the subject towns had no share in the central government; the idea of representation was almost entirely unknown. Since there were no constituents to whom politicians must account for their conduct, the responsibility of officials was obtained only by an elaborate system of checks and counter-checks amongst the branches of the administration, by extremely short periods and rapid rotation of office, by appointment by lot, and by what appears a most cumbersome system of "Colleges" and "Councils," without the consent of all of which very little could be accomplished. Parties were not vast organisations with common programmes; they were merely groups of individuals, held together by the family tie as much as by any common interests that they might chance to possess. It was the work of the politician therefore to deal with men only, not with organisations; with individual ambitions, not with party programmes.

Yet it is deeply interesting to observe how mediævalism still clung about every institution and coloured every circumstance. The family played the principal part in political grouping, there was still a tendency to regard it, rather than the individual, as the unit in the state; industry was still partially controlled by the Guild system; political institutions were all based upon mediæval forms of government, and they retained more or less of their mediæval complexion and limitations. For Florence had been originally simply a union of land-holders for the purpose of mutual defence, and, when it became a trading community, many of the ideas of its agrarian past lingered on in it; early in the fifteenth century taxation was still mainly based upon land, though that had long ceased to be the chief source of wealth.

The days of its existence as a trading community, struggling for bare life among powerful feudal neighbours, had left yet stronger traces upon Florence. The Guild was the original basis of political and social organisation;

the Guilds, or "Arts," as they were called, were divided into classes, according to their wealth and importance. Of these, the higher class consisted of the "Major Arts," seven in number,—the Guilds of the lawyers, bankers, merchants, manufacturers of woollen and of silken goods, doctors, and furriers. Beneath them were fourteen "Minor Arts," whose trades were less important and less lucrative; and below them again a fluctuating number of smaller guilds, whose industries were dependent upon those of the Major Arts. Each Art had its own elected officials, its Guild Hall, its coat-of-arms and banner, its independent statutes and organisation. The Major Arts had political predominance; accordingly we find that in the Magistracies they furnished the greater number of officials, while the Minor Arts contributed a smaller number, and the rest of the people none at all.

Co-existent with the Guild organisation for commercial was that of the "Quarters" for military purposes. In the days when the Florentines did their own fighting, the city had been organised into four divisions or "Quarters," subdivided into four "Companies," each "Company" furnishing its own quota to the City Militia, marching under its own "Gonfalon" or flag, led by its own Captain or "Gonfalonier." Now it was long since the Florentines had fought for themselves; their fighting was all done by professional soldiers, commanded by "Condottiere" Generals, and hired from all parts of Italy, or from still farther afield. Yet the old military, as well as the old commercial, divisions still left their traces in political organisation. The first Magistracy of the City, called the "Signory," was composed of nine members, eight of whom were known as the "Priors of the Arts," six being members of the Major, two of the Minor, Arts, while two were drawn from each Quarter of the town. The second Magistracy consisted of the sixteen "Gonfaloniers" of the "Companies." These two, with a third—the twelve "Buonuomini" (good men)—were called collectively Signory and Colleges, and formed theoretically the supreme legislative and executive body, while the Signory also occasionally sat as a supreme Court of Justice in causes of state.

The ninth and principal member of the Signory was the "Gonfalonier of Justice," who owed the origin of his existence to another phase in Florentine mediæval history—the period of the struggle of the people against the nobles. The feudal nobility, whose property surrounded the city, had been always at war with the burghers; the latter were finally victorious, and, in order to suppress the power of their old enemies in the country, they hit upon the plan of forcing them to live within the town, where they could be under constant supervision. The effect of this measure was merely to transfer the battlefield between the nobles and the people—"Grandi" and "Popolani"—from the country to the streets of the city itself. After long years of struggle, the "Popolani" triumphed; by the Ordinances of Justice of 1293 and onwards, the "Grandi" were deprived of nearly all political privileges, though a few posts, like that of ambassador, might be held by them, and they were placed under the restrictions of a severe criminal code. The Gonfalonier of Justice was the official originally appointed to execute the Ordinances; he had, as chief of the Signory, gradually become the most important official in Florence.

Another survival of the old days of warfare was the office of the "Captain of the People," who had originally acted as the leader of the Popòlani against the Grandi, and in later times exercised considerable judicial power, particularly in civil cases; but who was now little more than the head of a court of Summary Jurisdiction.

Yet another survival was the "Podestà," the foreign lawyer who, as a neutral, was called in to judge between the citizens. In the fifteenth century he still retained much criminal jurisdiction; we shall find later how his authority in the more important cases came to be superseded.

The Captain and the Podestà were severally Presidents of the two great Councils, that of the Captain or People, and that of the Podestà or Commune. Every measure passed by the Signory and Colleges had to be brought before them in turns for confirmation. The members of the Signory and Colleges themselves sat in both these Councils *ex officio*, as well as certain other officials. The Council of the People contained three hundred members, and since its President, the Captain, had been originally the chief officer of the people against the nobles, this council consisted wholly of members of the Arts; while in that of the Podestà, or Commune, consisting of two hundred and fifty persons, a certain number of nobles, or "Grandi," might take part.

For the "Grandi" class, though its *raison d'être* had long since disappeared, still existed in Florence. Its members were the principal landowners, and as such the principal tax-payers. Yet they were as a class excluded from all but a very insignificant share in the government. Of late years it had been found a convenient form of proscription to elevate opponents to the rank of nobles,—in fact, to "kick them upstairs."

The struggle between nobles and people had been but a part of the great thirteenth and fourteenth century contest between Guelfs and Ghibellins. The Guelfs, the party of the burghers, were victorious; during the time of strife they had formed themselves into an organisation for attack and defence, called the "Parte Guelfa." It had officials, statutes, and property of its own, and became as it were a corporation within the Corporation. When the Guelfs were victorious, the "Parte Guelfa" obtained the power to "ammunire," that is to say, to warn persons suspected of Ghibellinism from attempting to hold Government offices, and thus to deprive them of all part in politics. When Ghibellinism was practically extinct, this power was retained by the Parte Guelfa, which had fallen into the hands of a narrow oligarchy of the richer burghers, as a means to shut out from the Government all who did not belong to their faction. About 1378 there was a movement in the city to check the disastrous consequences of this tyrannical power, and to widen the Government; the leader of the movement was a respectable citizen of the middle class, Salvestro de' Medici. In order to obtain their desire, the supporters of the new movement called in the aid of the lower classes, and suddenly all the discontent of the disenfranchised class, oppressed both politically and industrially, broke into flame, and Florence was involved in a bloody war between labour and capital. The leaders of the original movement and their aims were swept aside; for some months Florence was in the hands of a turbid mob, which would not be content without obtaining a full share in the management of politics as a means to economic reform. They wanted industrial equality for all the Guilds, and suggested a sliding scale of taxation as a means to equalise wealth.

In a short time, however, the reaction came; the revolt was crushed, its principal leaders banished, and the oligarchy became almost as powerful and narrow as before. The lower classes were utterly excluded from the Government; the share of the Minor Arts in the Government offices was fixed at one-quarter, the Parte Guelfa nominally restored. Yet the real changes wrought by this "Ciompi" rebellion were very great. The power of the Guilds as political associations was really gone; the Parte Guelfa never recovered its authority, and in the fifteenth century it was nothing but a name.

Yet the Parte Guelfa had, during the years preceding the Ciompi rebellion, practically acted as the executive in Florence, and its place had to be filled. The nominal executive was quite incapable of performing its supposed functions. True, the power of the Signory was theoretically very great; it was supposed to have supreme control of the administration, and to be the sole initiator of legislation. Yet so careful had been the builders of the constitution to prevent its becoming too powerful, that they had left it practically incapable of independent action. Its members were drawn by lot, and a considerable period had to elapse before they could again hold office, so that many of them were personally unequal to their position. Its period of office was only two months, at the end of which time its members were liable to the revenge of any powerful faction that they had offended.

Its power was further limited by the necessity of getting nearly all its measures confirmed by the Colleges and Councils, and since two-thirds was the legal majority in all of these bodies, it may readily be conceived how slow and difficult a business was government. All these limitations and divisions of authority are the marks of a purely democratic constitution, but Florence was now in the hands of an oligarchy. The oligarchy had therefore to find means both to keep the executive entirely within its own control and to perform its functions for it; and so weak was it that the oligarchs, as long as they were united amongst themselves, found little difficulty in managing it. First it was necessary to make sure that no person could obtain any office of importance who was not a member of the ruling party, or could not be thoroughly trusted by it. Theoretically, all members of the Arts who had attained full age were qualified to hold office; but this privilege was limited by the necessity of passing what were called the "Scrutinies" for office. There were separate Scrutinies made for the Signory and the Colleges, for the lesser internal and for all the external offices; the names of those who had passed them were put into "borse" or purses, and there were separate "borse" for each of the offices which had to be filled. From these "borse" the names of the persons to hold office were drawn periodically by lot; for example, the names of the Signory were drawn every two months from the "borse" prepared for that purpose. The object of the Government was therefore to control the making of the Scrutinies; how this was done we cannot precisely ascertain, since we do not know who had the power to make the Scrutinies, though it was probably the Councils; but certainly there was voting on the subject, since those who wished to pass the Scrutiny canvassed for votes, and influential members of the Government could get those persons passed whom they privately favoured.

Again, it had long been the custom of the Signory to call upon a number of the leading citizens to give them advice and aid in important affairs. A Council thus held was called a "Pratica," the members of it "Richiesti." Under the oligarchy these informal "Pratiche" almost developed into a regular Council of Government. All the chief members of the ruling party sat on them; they were consulted on all important Government business, and though they preserved formal deference to the Signory, the advice which they gave it was practically a command.

And in order that foreign and military affairs might be capably conducted, the oligarchy created a new Council of ten persons, called the "Dieci," intended to imitate the more famous Venetian Council of Ten. The Dieci, who were all of the ruling party, were, however, only appointed in time of war; and though they considerably weakened the Signory by depriving it of some of its functions, they never obtained a permanent position or an authority like that of their Venetian prototype.

By all these means not only the executive was kept under control, but its action was made firm and rapid, and a continuity of policy was secured.

For many years the oligarchy ruled Florence successfully. During the latter years of the fourteenth century the strength of the Republic was strained to the uttermost in her conflict with Gian Galeazzo Visconti, the powerful and unscrupulous Duke of Milan. The strong executive needed to resist him successfully was found in the oligarchy. After his death the Republic accomplished one of the most brilliant feats in her history, the conquest of Pisa; and during the earlier years of the fifteenth century she was involved in another life-and-death struggle with Ladislas of Naples. At the death of Ladislas in 1414, the oligarchy was at the summit of its power. "One may rightly say," declares Guicciardini, the most impartial of all authorities, "that it was the wisest, the most glorious, the most happy government that our city has ever had." All foreign enemies were crushed, the territory of the Republic was increased by the addition of Pisa and Cortona; while the possession of Pisa gave Florence a new access to the sea, and filled her with ambitions to succeed to the naval power of the captured city. Small maritime undertakings prospered, although the greater enterprises patronised and managed by the Government were not so successful. Attempts were made to establish a comprehensive Eastern trade, a consul was sent to Alexandria, ships to the Morea and Ragusa. The western commerce of Florence was also advancing by huge strides; her exports to Venice alone were worth nearly a million ducats a year. In spite of the heavy expenses of the wars, the "Monti"—national stocks— had not gone down in value, and foreigners asked as a favour to be allowed to invest money in them.

The oligarchs had so far been held together by the pressure of foreign wars, and the fear of a repetition of the "Ciompi" rebellion, in which so many of their relatives perished. They were becoming an hereditary clique, to which certain families alone were admitted, and a tendency towards the descent of a position in the Government from father to son was beginning to gain ground. Thus, on the deaths of Maso degli Albizzi and of Matteo Castellani, their eldest sons, Rinaldo and Francesco, the latter only a child, were knighted with great ceremony by the Commune, as if to take their fathers' places. "The city of Florence," wrote a contemporary, "was at this time in the most happy condition, full of men gifted in every direction, each one trying to surpass the other in merit." Supreme amongst these were half a dozen men whose wealth, wisdom, and political experience enabled them to lead the others. These were Gino Capponi, the "Conqueror of Pisa," Lorenzo Ridolfi, Agnolo Pandolfini, Palla Strozzi, Matteo Castellani, Niccolò Uzzano—all men who took part in the Pratiche, conducted foreign embassies, sat in the Dieci, and frequently held other offices. But the chief of all was Maso degli Albizzi, whose ability and energy had enabled him to gain so commanding a position that it almost seemed as if before long the Rule of the Few might be converted into the Rule of One.

Yet when the pressure of war and the fear of a new "Ciompi" were removed, the oligarchy began to suffer from that weakness which sooner or later causes the ruin of all oligarchies—internal dissension. The least important of its members were jealous of the greater, and all were jealous of Maso degli Albizzi. The party began to split up in small cliques, mainly on family lines, each struggling for the supremacy. Maso's strong hand was removed in 1417, but even before his death there were signs that his supreme authority was not unquestioned. Gino Capponi had headed a party which objected to the last peace signed with Ladislas in 1414; Maso had the greatest difficulty in obtaining its confirmation by the Councils; Gino was even accused of a plot against Maso's life.

After Maso's death the nominal head of the Government was Niccolò Uzzano, an elderly man, cautious and experienced. Rinaldo degli Albizzi, Maso's son, a young man of great talents, who had already served an apprenticeship in most of the Government offices and in numerous foreign embassies, was probably ill-contented with Uzzano's supremacy, and there were others of the younger generation who showed signs of resenting the authority of the older and wiser heads. Yet for years it is impossible to find any organised opposition within the ranks of the ruling party,—only there was general discontent, and constant complaints of the want of union in the Government, and of the way in which public affairs were conducted by private cabals. Even the Pratiche were becoming shams, when Uzzano and his personal friends had decided before the Pratica met what policy they meant to adopt; and, after the uninitiated had been allowed to amuse themselves by airing their several opinions, Uzzano, who had apparently been asleep throughout the discussion, woke, stood up and explained his views, to which his followers immediately expressed their adhesion.

The disunion of the Government was the cause of the gradual, but steady, revival of those parties which had been crushed by the oligarchy after the suppression of the "Ciompi" rebellion. Chief amongst them were the members of the Minor Arts, who were excluded from all but a small share in the government; and also a great number of those members of the Major Arts who, though theoretically capable of office, were unable to pass the Scrutinies. Others again had passed the Scrutinies and could hold office, but yet were without influence in the Government, because they did not chance to belong to one of the families of which the ruling party was composed. The last quarter of a century had seen a great increase in the wealth of these excluded classes; they were already as rich as, or richer than, the members of the oligarchy, and naturally wished their political position to correspond with the social standing given them by their wealth.

They were by degrees reinforced by all the elements of discontent within the city. There were the Grandi, heavily taxed, and almost unrepresented in the Government; and there were the lower classes, who also thought themselves unfairly taxed, and whose interests the Government never seemed inclined to take into the smallest account in deciding any question of policy. Maso degli Albizzi had had the wisdom to conciliate this class by a popular economic policy, and personally he was much liked, but his successors did not continue in his steps. Yet it was long before these various elements could coalesce. At present there was only a good deal of discontent, slowly and steadily spreading; but there was nothing like a united party, nor was there any common leader.

The man to whom the popular party seems later to have turned for a head was Giovanni de' Medici, whose enormous wealth gave him both social and financial predominance in a commercial city like Florence. Giovanni was connected with that Salvestro de' Medici who was leader of the Moderates in 1378. Salvestro's branch of the family had been proscribed at that time, and members of it had been implicated in various later abortive revolts against the oligarchy. Vieri de' Medici had been offered the leadership of a popular rising in 1393, which he had wisely refused. Giovanni, who belonged to a branch of the family which had not fallen under the proscription, was equally cautious, and succeeded so well in avoiding all suspicion of disaffection that he obtained to the full the position to which his wealth and influence seemed to entitle him; he was admitted into the most intimate Pratiche of the Government, and held the most important offices, as Ambassador, on the Dieci, and as Gonfalonier. It was not until 1420, when the oligarchy was seriously divided within itself, that we find the least indication of any connection between him and what might be called the popular party, and then he acted together with Agnolo Pandolfini, one of the chief members of the oligarchy, as exponents of a popular "Peace Policy." Just afterwards he was Gonfalonier, but his period of office was not distinguished by any notable events. It is impossible to accuse him of having at this date any designs for supplanting the oligarchy, yet he was possibly already forming the nucleus of a personal following by means of the advantages which his wealth could confer.

The members of the oligarchy, instead of trying to strengthen their own hands or to disarm their enemies by prudent concessions, acted in the most shortsighted manner. In order to obtain a private following for the prosecution of their private feuds, they made individual allies amongst the discontented classes, many of whom had wealth and social importance. Their support was secured by getting their names passed through the Scrutinies and inserted in the Borse for the various Government offices, so that by this means the number of persons who obtained a share in the official government was rapidly increasing. Their private ambitions blinded the oligarchs to this widening of the ranks of the Government, and the consequent diminution of their own power as a party. Only Niccolò Uzzano seems to have understood what was going on, and discerned the probable results. In some verses addressed to the members of his party, he urged them to cease their private contests, and unite to withstand the upstarts who were pressing into the Government. "If you do not," he wrote, "soon you will be driven from the Halls of the Palace, and the privilege of using its staircase will be taken from you" (the Palace of the Signory, in which were the Government offices and council chambers, and whose stairs would chiefly be used by members of the Government). "These new people," he complained, "are already so powerful in the Court of the Palace and in the votes which they can command that little less than all the government is theirs. Before two more vintages have come and gone they will have seized all the authority." Uzzano's prophecy was a little premature, but it was none the less correct. The remedy which he suggested shows that he at least understood one of the true sources of weakness in the present Government, the failure of its power to control the official executive. So long as the oligarchs had been united amongst themselves this had not been difficult, but directly disunion weakened their solidarity, and they allowed persons who were not really in sympathy with them to penetrate into the offices, the uncertainty of their control became manifest.

For some time past we find that the Councils of the Popolo and Commune had not been well in hand. A great number of their members were officials, sitting in right of their office, and supposed to be devoted to the Government. Besides this, no freedom of debate was permitted in the Councils, and the voting was public. Yet as early as 1411 we find the Government creating two new Councils,—as if there were not already enough in Florence,—which were to be consulted in all foreign and military affairs. They were probably intended to act as a counterpoise to the older Councils. One had two hundred, the other a hundred and thirty-one members; they were accordingly called the Councils of Two Hundred and of a Hundred and Thirty-One; both were largely composed of Government officials; all the members must have passed the Scrutinies for Signory or Colleges. But even the Council of Two Hundred was not always amenable; we find it refusing twenty-six times to confirm a peace with Ladislas of Naples.

That which Uzzano chiefly blamed was the extension of the limits of the Scrutiny, and the consequent admission of independent elements into the offices. To remedy this he proposed to have recourse to what was looked upon as an extraordinary measure in Florentine politics, only to be resorted to on critical occasions,—the holding of a Parliament. In its origin the Parliament was based on the same idea as the modern Plebiscite, the reference of a matter of supreme importance to an assembly of the whole community. At the ringing of the great bell of the Palace, all the citizens were supposed to gather in the principal square where the Palace stood. The Signory came out upon the "Ringhiera," or balcony, of the Palace, and made proposals to the assembled multitude, upon which they gave their opinion by acclamation. But the ceremony had long since passed into a mere form for carrying through a considerable change in the Government. On the pretence of maintaining order, the square was carefully guarded by armed men under the command of the party in power; only a few people, and these not necessarily qualified citizens, ventured to appear, probably expecting to get a *pour-boire* for their complaisance. When the Chancellor of the Signory inquired if at least two-thirds of the citizens were present, they shouted cheerfully "Yes! Yes!" and to every proposal of the Signory read out by him afterwards the answer was the same. The proposal usually made was for the appointment of a Balìa,—that is to say, a large Committee of two or three hundred persons known to be favourable to the Government,—and to them was given almost absolute power to "reform" the city as they pleased, and principally to make new Scrutinies. Such an instrument as the power to hold a Parliament would, of course, have enabled the Signory who dared have recourse to it to carry through any change in the Government that they pleased; but no Signory would dare to call a Parliament, unless they were certain of the support—and armed support—of a very powerful party in the city. No doubt, if Uzzano's advice had been taken at the time, and a Parliament held by the oligarchy, they would have been able to create a Balìa, which should make new Scrutinies, excluding from office all those whose fidelity to the Government was doubtful; but the oligarchs themselves were too busy with their private feuds and ambitions to be able to agree on a measure of such importance; the very fact that Uzzano advised a Parliament would have been enough to make a large section of the party most unwilling to consent to it.

Yet, so long as the peace and prosperity continued which Florence had enjoyed since 1414, the weight of taxation did not press heavily upon the people, and there were no dangerous contests; but about 1420 there arose a new question of foreign policy, which divided all Florence into two opposing camps, the Peace party and the War party. The War party contained most of the older and wiser politicians, like Gino Capponi, who were anxious, by a bold and decisive policy, to hold in check the ever growing and threatening power of Filippo Maria Visconti, the young Duke of Milan. The Peace party was, however, the most popular. The "people" disliked war and an adventurous foreign policy. They were "little Florentiners"; they did not care about opening up distant markets, as did the greater merchants; they were absolutely indifferent to the intangible advantages of honour and glory; all that they wanted was peace, prosperity at home, and low taxation. And we find the names of Giovanni de' Medici and Agnolo Pandolfini put forward as exponents of their views. A party in the Government was indeed willing to promote its own interests by truckling to the popular outcry; and, instead of assisting

Genoa to withstand Visconti's attacks, a treaty was made between Florence and Milan, which gave Visconti the leisure to conquer Genoa, from whence he threatened Tuscany on the north-west. Almost immediately afterwards he broke this treaty, which had bound him not to interfere in Romagna, and, invading that district, seized Forlì and Imola, both of which towns were "raccomandati" to, that is, under the protection of, Florence. The Peace party still urged that Romagna, where, on account of the Papal suzerainty, it was impossible for Florence to acquire proprietary rights, should be left to its fate, and that Florence should only defend her own territory; but the War party, pointing out the fatal mistake that had been committed in allowing Visconti to absorb Genoa, succeeded in making Florence declare war and invade Romagna.

The war was, on the whole, unsatisfactory. Visconti easily beat Florence alone; and even when Florence was joined with Venice, it was the latter only that reaped the benefit of their joint successes. Peace was concluded in 1428; Florence gained nothing from it but barren honour, though she had succeeded in checking Visconti's ambitions. But she had had to pay dear for this success. War had continued for four years; three and a half million florins had been spent upon it. The city was impoverished, the governing party had become unpopular and seriously divided within itself. The blame for every failure was, of course, thrown upon those who had counselled the rupture of peace, and those members of the governing party who had from the first declared against the war had now formed themselves into a regular opposition. The League with

Venice, which necessitated a continuation of war, was forced through the Councils with great difficulty.

War taxation had begun to press very heavily upon the poor, used to many years of "Peace Budgets." The money voted could not be collected: "The powerful refuse to pay, and the others follow their example." Rinaldo degli Albizzi himself admitted that "the people are in great affliction." The general distress was increased by a series of commercial failures consequent upon the war. A heavy tax, called the Ventina, because its assessment was in the hands of twenty (venti) citizens, was levied in 1426 in a most arbitrary fashion. It met with disfavour from rich and poor alike. It had already become obvious to the more enlightened members of the Government that a change in the distribution of taxation was absolutely necessary if they were to hold the reins of power any longer. Niccolò Uzzano had admitted this as early as 1424, but he wished to defer the change for a time. The ancient methods had indeed long ago been out of date; they were originally made to suit a land-owning community, and there was no sufficient provision for the taxation of mercantile gains, which were in Florence the chief source of wealth. By the old system of taxation, called the Estimo, officials appointed by the Government for the purpose made an arbitrary assessment of the supposed income of the tax-payers; and while the proprietors of land were highly rated, the possessors of movable goods, securities, and ready-money came off easily. There was also a poll-tax which fell heavily upon the poor; and while the Grandi—the principal landowners—and such rich persons as were disliked by the

Government, and were consequently rated highly by the assessors, shared the weight of the burden, the majority of wealthy merchants, of whom the governing party was composed, were lightly taxed. Sometimes impositions of the Estimo were reckoned as loans, and received interest at the "Monte Comune"; but these loans were forced, and the interest not very regularly paid. Arrears in the payment of taxes were punished by exclusion from office, and sometimes by severer penalties. Some fixed rate of taxation, and one that would touch the real sources of wealth, was required; but it was not likely that the governing class, who benefited by the old system, would consent to such a reformation, unless forced to it by a dire sense of its necessity. Yet, since the beginning of 1425, Rinaldo degli Albizzi himself and a few others of his party, convinced that the present system must lead to their ultimate ruin,—probably to another great revolution,—had been urging in the Government councils the adoption of a system known as the "Catasto." It was used successfully at Venice; and Venice was the model which the oligarchy always held up before itself for imitation. "It is impossible," Rinaldo exclaimed, "for the citizens to bear these great burdens unless their distribution is equal; which it is not, since some pay fifty soldi in the pound, some only ten." Rinaldo believed that equality of taxation would put an end to the civil discords, by putting an end to so fruitful a cause of quarrel.

The disturbances which followed the imposition of the "Ventina" brought up the question again. The attempts of the tax-gatherers to collect the money were in some cases met by forcible resistance; riots ensued, and civil war threatened. In the summer of 1426 Rinaldo was again pressing the introduction of the Catasto. For some months after this he was absent from Florence on foreign embassies; the subject was not forgotten during his absence, but after his return it was put forward more forcibly than before; Niccolò Uzzano had been converted to support it, though not very enthusiastically. The force of public opinion had now become too strong for the waverers. In May 1427 the scheme of the Catasto was drawn up, and a committee appointed to put it into force.

This committee was to demand from every householder an exact account of his sources of income from fixed and movable goods, business profits, credits, government securities,—that is to say, money in the "Monti,"—and ready-money. The income derived from house property was to be estimated by its rent, that from land by the current market value of its products. After verifying as nearly as possible and registering all these,—inspecting, for example, the books of merchants to see if their account of their business profits was correct,— the Committee were to capitalise every person's income at the rate of 7 per cent; that is to say, each person who had seven florins of income was supposed to have a hundred of capital. Each imposition of the tax was at the rate of $\frac{1}{2}$ per cent on the capital thus estimated, that is, a fourteenth part of the income; but, as the Catasto was usually demanded several times in the course of a year, a very considerable proportion would have been paid, had not large deductions been made from the capital for what were considered the necessaries of life before the tax was laid upon it. The dwelling-house and shop came under this category; so also did their necessary furniture and utensils, and a certain sum for their repair and maintenance; so too did the animals and tools employed in business or labour, bad debts, obligations by will, and two hundred florins a year for the maintenance of each member of the family, not including servants. Hence the tax fell only upon what was considered the superabundance, and the income of the majority did not reach the taxable sum. Of these persons, those who had a certain amount of property had to pay a small tax, fixed by composition with the Committee; while all,—those who paid the Catasto and those who did not,—had to pay a small graduated poll-tax of from two to six soldi. The Registers were to remain in force for three years, and then be revised to suit the shiftings of property which would have taken place in that period. This was accordingly done in 1431.

The immediate result of the Catasto was largely to increase the contributions paid by members of the Government. For example, instead of making small nominal payments, Palla Strozzi, Giovanni de' Medici, and Niccolò Uzzano were now rated severally at 500, 300, and 200 florins. But with the poorer classes, who benefited considerably, the reform was popular; we hear that "it pleased the people greatly." Yet it was not the Government or Rinaldo who won the credit for what had been done. It was believed to be only a measure of conciliation to which they had been forced, by the pressing necessity to give way on this point, or to surrender their power altogether. So far the popular opinion was on the whole correct, but it was quite incorrect in ascribing the real credit of the measure to a person who deserved no credit for it whatever,—who had, in fact, been rather unfavourable to it than otherwise,—to Giovanni de' Medici. According to the records of the meetings of the Pratiche, Giovanni took very little part in urging the Catasto. Once, when the subject first came forward, he spoke in general terms, recommending an equality of taxation; but when the Catasto was being discussed in detail, he spoke only with hesitation : " Very many have recommended the Catasto; some doubt what fruit will come of it. If it can be carried out it will be useful, but he himself cannot say whether it will bear fruit or no." Yet a popular tradition certainly did credit him with the introduction of the Catasto. If this tradition is to be believed, we must suppose that he was dissembling his real feelings in this speech, while privately encouraging the popular agitation. But it is to be noted how much his own rate of taxation was increased by the new system.

But the Catasto did not bring peace : the root of civil discord lay still deeper down. Its immediate effect was to alienate many supporters and hangers-on of the Government, who had benefited pecuniarily by the old system, and who now had to pay heavy taxes. Many business men also strongly objected to the publicity entailed by having to show their books to the Catasto committee. The populace, far from showing gratitude, demanded that the Catasto should be made retrospective, that is to say, that the rich should be made to pay now all they would have paid had the Catasto been established some years previously. Personal struggles between cliques in the Government and the agitation of the unenfranchised classes did not cease. One of the greatest difficulties with which the Government had to contend was the prevalence of secret political societies, which, under pretence of being religious confraternities, met in the churches for the purpose of agitation and intrigue. Numerous laws were passed for their suppression; one speaker in the Catasto debates declared that the new system of taxation would put an end to "secret societies, the power of cliques, and the quarrels of the people," but his hope was disappointed. The societies continued to exist, and to hold their secret meetings. In order to check the growing strength of the Minor Arts, Rinaldo, it was confidently asserted, with how much truth it is now difficult to judge, proposed to his party a scheme for reducing the number of these Arts from fourteen to seven, and diminishing their share in the government proportionately. It was rumoured that this plan was frustrated by the opposition of Giovanni de' Medici. The failures of the war increased the unpopularity of the Government; yet one chronicler declared that, had not military affairs somewhat distracted popular attention from internal politics, "the heads of at least four prominent persons would have been cut off every year."

The existence of a secret political intrigue within the Government itself is revealed to us by the sudden and unexplained dismissal in 1427 of Pagolo Fortini, Chancellor of the Signory. A few months later, Martino Martini, Notary of the Riformagioni,[1] was also dismissed.

[1] The Riformagioni was the Florentine Record Office, by which all new laws and decisions were registered. The Notary of the Riformagioni and the Chancellor of the Signory were amongst the few permanent officials of the Republic.

The exact significance of these events it is difficult to determine. Interested witnesses declared in after years that Giovanni de' Medici procured the fall of Fortini, hoping to follow it up by a political *coup d'état* and the banishment of Uzzano; but that his plan failed, Uzzano escaped, and was able to retaliate by the dismissal of Martini, who was a political agent of the Medici. There is no doubt that Martini was the close ally of the Medici in the intrigues of the next few years, yet he was also closely connected with Rinaldo degli Albizzi both before and after this time; so that if a plot against Uzzano were really in contemplation, Rinaldo must either have been neutral or of the Medicean party. There are certainly signs that Rinaldo had at this time formed a political alliance with the Medici in opposition to Uzzano and the older members of the Government. We find him immediately after the fall of Fortini writing in the most intimate, even affectionate, terms to Giovanni's nephew, Averardo de' Medici, and speaking of his cousin as "thy Cosimo, to whom all my désire is known." And Rinaldo was a man who "did not know how to feign."

Just after Martini's dismissal Giovanni de' Medici died, whether from grief at the failure of his plans or not we cannot say. His part in the politics of the last few years it is extremely difficult to determine. From official sources of information we learn nothing of importance about him. It is possible that after his death, and after Cosimo's accession to supreme power, a kind of legend was formed concerning him, and his name connected with a popular agitation in which he really had no share. It is more probable, as the apologists of his family assert, that the fragmentary portions of the popular party, gradually reorganising themselves, and gaining in political power and significance, strove to make Medici with his popular name become their leader, and that he held back. According to tradition, upon his deathbed he gave his sons the advice never to "use the Palace of the Government as if it were your place of business; wait to go there until you are sent for; only receive such favours from the people as are freely bestowed; never make a show before the people, or, if you must, let it be the least possible." Yet it seems almost certain that Giovanni himself, while avoiding public notoriety, was silently helping to re-establish and organise a popular party, to be led by himself or his sons. There seems no doubt that, with his vast wealth and commercial connections, he was gradually purchasing individual adherents by pecuniary favours, by assistance in business, or an actual gift of money, with which the recipient might pay off his taxes and obtain office in the Republic. His generosity to the Church and in almsgiving increased Giovanni's personal popularity.

At his death all this wealth and influence passed to his eldest son, Cosimo, who was then in the prime of life, thirty-nine years of age, and already a figure of some importance in political circles. As a boy he had seen military service at the siege of Pisa; when quite a young man he had accompanied Pope John XXII. as his financial agent to the Council of Constance, since his father was the Pope's banker. On the flight of the Pope, Cosimo left Constance in disguise, and travelled for a time in France and Germany, returning to Florence in 1416. A partisan said afterwards that he undertook this journey in order to escape notice and divert the jealous suspicions of the governing party; and that after his return to Florence he lived in retirement, and avoided politics as much as possible for the same reason. But it does not appear that the Government was much afraid of him, or that he was very retiring, since during the next twelve years he was twice a member of the Signory, was employed on embassies to Milan, Lucca, and Bologna, and in 1426 was entrusted alone with a mission of considerable importance to the Pope. Cosimo had one younger brother, Lorenzo, with whom he was on excellent terms; but the political importance of the younger was entirely absorbed in that of the elder brother.

To any one able to fish in troubled waters Florence presented excellent opportunities. The Catasto had been of no use in checking dissensions, which were as rife as ever; while the Peace of 1428 caused public attention to be turned entirely upon home affairs. A new office had just been established with a view to securing the better administration of public functions,—that of the Conservators of the Laws, who were to exercise a much-needed supervision over Government officials. It was a good measure, but, like the Catasto, did not reach the root of the matter. The attempt to suppress secret political societies had been a failure, for they were still in existence everywhere; complaints against them were numerous at the Pratiche, held frequently in 1429 to discuss the possibility of "restoring unity" in the distracted city. The outcome of these meetings was a new law; "Lex contra Scandalosos" it was called, but the Florentines readily changed its name into the "Scandalous Law." By it was created a large committee, who were to receive complaints against persons considered "scandalous," the disturbers of peace, or those "who wish to be more powerful than the Commune itself"; to discuss such charges, and, if proved, to punish the accused by fine or banishment. This law only led to worse confusion, more intrigues and quarrels than before. It was hardly ever put into force, but the threat of its action did more harm than good.

Meanwhile the opponents of the Catasto, in order to make it as odious as possible, had extended it to those subject towns of Florence which considered themselves to have a right to settle their own taxation. This led to a rebellion at Volterra, which was only suppressed by force.

Immediately afterwards an opportunity occurred for an attack upon the neighbouring state of Lucca, whose ruler, Paolo Guinigi, had for some time seemed ill-disposed towards Florence. Uzzano, Agnolo Pandolfini, Palla Strozzi, and all the wiser heads were strongly opposed to a new war. Florence, they pointed out, had not recovered from the financial strain of the war with Milan—"the ink is hardly yet dry upon the terms of peace"; Guinigi had himself just offered to make a league with Florence. The attack on Lucca would rouse the jealousy of Siena, which would think that Florence meant to turn upon her next; above all, Visconti would eagerly look out for the moment when Florence, embarrassed by a Lucchese war, should be unable to resist him, in order to renew his aggressions upon Romagna.

But a violent popular agitation had broken out in favour of war. The introduction of the Catasto had quite changed the views of the lower classes upon foreign policy. They now believed that money would be easily forthcoming, but not out of their pockets; and the people assembled in crowds in the streets to make demonstrations in favour of war. The popular cry was taken up by some of the younger members of the oligarchy, especially by Rinaldo degli Albizzi and Neri Capponi, the brilliant young son of the famous Gino, now dead. They hoped to obtain popularity for themselves, and they expected that the conquest of Lucca would give them the prestige that their fathers had gained by the conquest of Pisa. No doubt too they hoped to distract the minds of the people from domestic politics; "it was all done," said a contemporary, "to lead the people under the yoke." Therefore they declared that the acquisition of Lucca was necessary as a defence to Pisa, and as a bulwark against Visconti's encroachments. After a fortnight's disputing, Albizzi's party gained the day; in a united assembly of all the Councils the war was approved by a majority of four to one. Neri Capponi was a member of the first Dieci appointed; Rinaldo was one of the War Commissioners sent to the camp (December 1429).

From the first, however, the Peace party were determined that the war should not succeed, lest success should give too much power to those who had advocated it; and they intrigued in every way possible against the War Commissioners, and did all they could to hamper their progress. The Commissioners, even Rinaldo, were anxious above everything to maintain their personal reputation in Florence, and spent their energies in justifying themselves in letters home rather than in attacking Lucca. Yet so badly was Rinaldo treated, harried by directions and counter-directions, kept short of supplies, upbraided for failing to obtain great victories, that his three months' service at the camp was one long torment. He exclaimed to a friend, "I know now how these tongues of the Florentines are made! Who has regard to them will never do anything of use to the Commune!" Finally, Rinaldo's authority was practically superseded by the despatch of two additional Commissioners to the camp, Neri Capponi and Alamanno Salviati. This Rinaldo bitterly resented, and the rivalry between him and Neri, which was perhaps inherited from their respective fathers, now became very acute. They had both desired war, but each wished for all the crédit of any success achieved in it. Neri appropriated the whole merit of their few conquests, and when Rinaldo seemed about to obtain a success, endeavoured to frustrate him. Neri was an intimate friend of the Condottiere general, Fortebraccio, then employed by Florence; and they acted together, disregarding Rinaldo's advice and wishes.

So powerful was Neri's influence with the troops that Rinaldo declared that "if anything" (*i.e.* a revolution) "should happen in Florence—from which God preserve us—and Neri should be found here with this reputation and following, he would be able to do anything that he pleased." Rinaldo meant that he would be able to lead the army against Florence, and seize the government of the city. After Neri's return to Florence, Rinaldo found Alamanno Salviati no less difficult to deal with. Alamanno took the best of everything, and claimed all credit for himself, while doing absolutely nothing to deserve it. At last Rinaldo obtained his own recall to Florence, and hastened home to justify himself before the Dieci, who, in his presence, seem to have had no definite charge to make against him (March 1430).

A few years later, when the crisis of the Medici fortunes arrived, Cosimo and his cousin, Averardo de' Medici, were accused of having stirred up the Lucchese war, in order to introduce strife and dissension into the city and bring Florence into financial distress for their own profit. Again, they were supposed, for the same reasons, to have done all they could to prevent and delay the conclusion of the war. Averardo was charged with getting Neri Capponi sent to the camp to embarrass Rinaldo, and with intriguing to prevent either Neri or Rinaldo from achieving any military successes. Cosimo was charged with aiding and abetting these proceedings, but not as the principal mover in them. There is, however, no proof to be found in the private letters of the cousins to one another of any such designs. In 1430, Cosimo was away from Florence to escape an epidemic of the plague; he wrote his opinions quite openly to Averardo: "It appears to me that, this undertaking having pleased the majority of the people, and affairs having reached a condition in which the honour of the Republic is involved, each one ought now to favour it as much as possible, and thus I shall do as much as I can here, and advise you to do the same." Later he bewailed the misfortunes which had been caused by the bad management of the war. "It will last longer than we hoped," he wrote, "and all because we would not when we could. May God pardon them that were the cause!" There could have been no object in shamming such sentiments as these to Averardo, his supposed fellow-conspirator. Cosimo's intimate and trusted friend, Puccio Pucci, a rising young politician, had spoken strongly in the Pratiche against the war.

Averardo, however, was a shifty person, who probably intrigued with both parties at once. He and Martino Martini, the Medici agent, were, from the beginning of the war, openly allied with Rinaldo, who was on the look-out for supporters against the Peace party. They were all opposed to Neri Capponi, Capponi and Martini leading opposite factions in the Dieci. Rinaldo corresponded intimately with Averardo, who was in command at Pisa, addressing him as "thou," and he evidently looked upon Martini as his friend and supporter. He bade his son keep Martini posted in all his affairs. "Let him know everything," he wrote, "he is a very useful man; he is our friend." Rinaldo's son wrote to Averardo, "I trust in you as in a father," while Rinaldo constantly complained to Averardo of the treatment that he endured from Neri Capponi and Alamanno Salviati, receiving sympathetic replies. Yet Averardo was hardly an honest friend to Rinaldo. Alamanno was his own son-in-law, and he certainly listened as much to Alamanno's complaints of Rinaldo as to Rinaldo's complaints of Averardo.

Meanwhile the war continued with signal ill-success; and after Rinaldo's retirement from the camp, things went from bad to worse. "Every day," wrote the Dieci themselves, "the reputation of our office and of this undertaking is declining, and the murmuring and complaining of the citizens increases." Amongst the members of a new Dieci elected in the summer were

Uzzano, Palla Strozzi, and Giovanni Guicciardini, all of whom had been from the first opposed to the war, while Guicciardini was even Commissioner at the camp. It was not likely that much would be accomplished under such management. Strozzi was actually lamenting loudly in the councils that there had ever been a war at all. Rinaldo still defended it. "The Lucchese expedition was rightly undertaken," he said. "If it does not respond to our hopes, we ought rather to inquire whence the defect arises than to blame the authors of the undertaking." But another counsellor maintained that it would be only just if those who had wished for the war should now be made to pay the cost of it! Every one was anxious to avoid responsibility and consequent blame. Cosimo wrote that neither he nor his brother wished to be members of the Dieci, since "I do not believe that the war can succeed, and would therefore rather be out of it altogether."

Nor could the war be confined to Lucca. Siena was negotiating with Guinigi, and then began to make raids on the Florentine borders; Genoa and the Pope were joining in the League against Florence, nor was Visconti likely to remain out of it long. Lorenzo de' Medici was sent to Milan to persuade him to let Tuscan affairs settle themselves, but the opportunity to embarrass Florence was too attractive. He sent a young Condottiere general, Francesco Sforza, to Lucca, who drove off the Florentine troops, carried through a revolution in the city in the interests of Visconti, deposing Guinigi and forming Lucca into a Republic, and finally allowed Florence to buy him off for 50,000 florins. "A needless expense," wrote Cosimo, "since in any case he could not have remained at Lucca, as the plague was destroying his army, and he could get no provisions." His place was taken by a yet more formidable Condottiere, Piccinino, who completely defeated the Florentine army, and by the summer of 1431 was threatening Pisa. Things would have gone ill with Florence had not a new war between Venice and Visconti forced the latter to withdraw his troops from Tuscany. All these misfortunes had made the state of affairs within Florence worse than ever. Rinaldo acknowledged that "the peril is great, but all the more necessary is it to provide against it." He was answered by the usual angry reproaches against those who had begun the war. Only Averardo de' Medici supported him, saying, "Things are against us, but we ought not to lose heart." Cosimo, in fact, had just written to him, congratulating him that matters "were no worse" than they were: "and indeed it seems to me that there has been very little provision on our part" to meet dangers.

But it was difficult now to encourage Florence to fresh efforts. When the war began she was conscious of the possession of great resources, but all these seemed to be exhausted. Her finances were in confusion, her courage consequently gone. All the bankers, but the Medici, refused to lend money upon public credit; the price of the Monte Comune fell very low. The Dieci and Commissioners did not cease to fling accusations at one another; Giovanni Guicciardini was recalled, and had to stand his trial for mismanagement as Commissioner.

The meetings of the Pratiche were mere scenes of

mutual recrimination. Discussions about the war had rendered the contests between the members of the governing party more bitter than ever. Lorenzo Ridolfi remarked that all these attacks on the authors of the war revealed only the discord within the city, "and this our enemies know, and it gives them boldness against us." Uzzano went near the root of the matter when he said that the cause of the discontent was "to see some in higher dignities than they are worthy of, and others kept under." But his suggested remedy showed the fatal weakness of his discrimination. "Justice ought to be done, and dignities given to those who merit them *on account of their families*." It seemed impossible to find a satisfactory remedy. In 1429, on the proposal of Lorenzo Ridolfi, a great meeting of citizens was held, at which all swore peace with one another upon the Book of the Gospels. This plan was tried again in April 1430, but quite as fruitlessly.

At last, early in 1432, Neri Capponi was banished on a frivolous pretext under the "Scandalous Law," but was immediately recalled by the next Signory. Rinaldo has been accused of compassing this as a private revenge, but Rinaldo was out of Florence at the time. Besides, he had often spoken of the law with severe disapproval, and Rinaldo's actions, even his attacks upon his enemies, had always been open and above board.

From that time, for a year, we hear very little of the internal affairs of Florence. No more Pratiche for "promoting unity" were held, perhaps because unity was now considered hopeless. Foreign affairs distracted the minds of the leading citizens; they were busy with elaborate negotiations. Many were absent from Florence for some months on embassies connected with the forthcoming peace. Military affairs were more prosperous: Michele Sforza, cousin of the more famous Francesco, gained a few small successes as Florentine Condottiere, while a Genoese fleet was defeated by some Venetian and Pisan ships. The advent of the Emperor Sigismund in Italy, whither he had come to obtain the Italian and Imperial Crowns, and his partisanship with Visconti, Siena, and Lucca, further complicated matters. Rinaldo was ambassador at Siena to treat for peace through the Emperor's mediation, but the negotiation failed. Palla Strozzi and Cosimo de' Medici were at the same time present at general negotiations which were going on at Ferrara between Milan, Venice, and Florence. Visconti, however, broke off the treaty, and Cosimo returned to Florence to serve a second time upon the Dieci. At last, in April 1433, a general peace was concluded. Strozzi was the Florentine envoy who signed it. Florence, Lucca, and Siena were all to restore conquests made at each other's expense. Florence, therefore, obtained nothing whatever by the war but heavy debts and general financial embarrassment, and, what was yet worse, her internal discords had increased to such an extent that the long dreaded crisis arrived only five months after the cessation of the war.

CHAPTER II

THE BANISHMENT AND RESTORATION OF COSIMO DE' MEDICI

THE aspect of affairs had changed very much since the days when the oligarchy was at the height of its power, and when a Florentine historian could write that "the city was in perfect peace and quiet, without the smallest cloud in the heavens." The change, as we have seen, was due to two main causes, the breaking up of the oligarchical party within itself, its internal quarrels and rivalries, and the gradual rise of a middle-class party, led by men of wealth and ability, some of whom had nominally full political privileges, but little opportunity to exercise them, and some who, as members of the Minor Arts, were almost excluded from political life. To them, as the party of the discontented, joined themselves all those who had private grievances against any particular member of the Government, and the Grandi and lower classes, who were shut out of politics altogether. For a long time these parties had been formless, unorganised, without leaders, only attracting notice by noisy complaints and resistance to the collection of taxes; but by degrees the different elements began to coalesce, as they found their grievances similar and their enemies identical. The influence that they had already obtained was shown by their success in forcing the Government to grant the Catasto, but what they really wanted was a share in political power. The Grandi had not forgotten the importance of their remote ancestors; the middle class recalled certain moments of the "Ciompi" period, when they had been the rulers of Florence.

The oligarchs, wrapped up in their personal pride and private squabbles, had been long in recognising the danger which threatened them, and when they did see it were too much divided amongst themselves to act with a strong hand all together. They preferred to make personal adherents amongst the discontented classes, and to use them as instruments against each other in their faction fights. Rinaldo was one of the few who believed that, to maintain the position of the oligarchy, concessions must be made to some of their opponents. He hoped to gain the lower classes by the Catasto and the Lucchese war, and, according to one chronicler at least, he had already suggested to his party an alliance with the Grandi against the Minor Arts, a suggestion he was to bring forward more forcibly later on. The Catasto failed to accomplish the purpose for which it was intended, and only succeeded in disintegrating yet further the broken ranks of the oligarchy. The Government was at the height of its unpopularity in 1433, when a disadvantageous peace closed a most dishonourable war—a war which one chronicler declares was "by permission of the gods, and because of our sins," and which was over and over again asserted to have been "the origin of the ruin of the city." The Florentines were easily discouraged by misfortune; "at every little reverse they give themselves up for lost," said a poet of their own; the long-continued hostilities had really caused much financial distress, while the disagreements about the management of the war had much increased the personal enmities amongst the members of the Government.

But in 1433 we find the position of persons and politics almost entirely reversed from what they had been in 1430; and the exact cause of this change it is difficult to arrive at. In 1430, Rinaldo degli Albizzi was allied with the Medici, and his principal enemy was Neri Capponi; he was also opposed, though less violently, to the party of old-fashioned politicians, Uzzano, Agnolo Pandolfini, etc. In 1433 Uzzano was dead, Pandolfini and Lorenzo Ridolfi were beginning to retire from politics; Neri Capponi seemed to occupy a neutral position between two parties, waiting to see which would win, in order that he might attach himself to the victors. Rinaldo was no longer afraid of him, all his enmity was now turned against the Medici, who had become the only objects of his fear and hatred. Rinaldo was by character a jealous man, a man who wished to be first, or nothing, but he was not calculated to be a party leader. He had many of the best qualifications of a citizen; he was active and energetic, ready to endure any hardships for the sake of the city, if not willing to deny himself the satisfaction of grumbling about them. He was courageous. "If," he wrote of himself, "I had but half the courage with which God has endowed me, I should yet think myself a brave man." He was singularly upright in a city full of intrigue. "I do not know how to pretend!" he exclaimed, and again, "I never belonged to any secret society, nor carried on any political business except in the Palace." He was generous too where the Republic was concerned. "The Commune owes me a certain quantity of money in payment of my official services," he wrote to the assessors of the Catasto, "but I do not esteem it as anything." But he had the worst qualifications for a leader: he was hard and unsympathetic, rather feared than loved; his very rectitude of character made him unpopular; he had none of his father's gift of making friends. Agnolo Pandolfini "could not endure him, because of his unbearable behaviour, and seeing of what evil he was the reason." Though possessing some political insight, he had not the power to convince other people of his views. He was impatient of blame, always feverishly anxious to justify his actions, painfully sensitive to public opinion; and though he wrote once, "My back is hardened now, and, doing my duty, I think little of the words of the wicked," he was in reality far from such a desirable state of mind. Impatient of advice, he was yet easily managed by those who knew how to work on his jealousy. "A man without fear," wrote a contemporary, "by whom great authority was worthily exercised. He was upright, eloquent, and so just and severe as by his enemies to be called cruel. He lived simply and sparingly, so that the envious said he was avaricious. Would to God that this man could not have been called proud!" Yet his chief fault was his fickleness of purpose. "He had no firmness nor constancy, any more than has a swallow in the air. . . .

He was full of an incomprehensible ill-temper, nor could he ever make up his mind to which party to belong. Sometimes he seemed all for the Medici, at other times all for Uzzano; so that as time is measured by hours and moments, even so often did he change party. Many said that he did not himself know what he wished, but . . . all these fox-like turns and twists were really made because he desired to be head of a party and leader of the people."

Hence the change of the object of his enmity from Neri to Cosimo, which was caused by his jealousy at the great increase of Cosimo's importance between the years 1430 and 1433. In 1430, Cosimo became a member of the Dieci, and, in spite of his efforts, Rinaldo never succeeded in getting himself elected to that office during the Lucchese war. In 1432, Cosimo shared with Palla Strozzi the very important peace negotiations at Ferrara; immediately after his return to Florence, he was again placed on the Dieci, and this office only ended in the spring of 1433. His great abilities were securing the acknowledgment they deserved; it almost seemed as if he was to fill the place as prudent and moderate counsellor which Uzzano had left empty.

But Cosimo's increased importance suggested more than this to Rinaldo, and not to Rinaldo only. His name made him heir to the old tradition of popular leadership, heir to Salvestro de' Medici; it recalled the Ciompi times, and suggested the restoration of the lower middle classes to a share in the government. Cosimo was seized upon as their natural head by all those groups of discontented people, who were merely needing a leader to unite them into a powerful party.

The party might in scorn be nicknamed "Puccini," from Puccio Pucci, but Rinaldo knew that it was really Cosimo who was dangerous. It was therefore natural that Rinaldo should fix upon him as his enemy. Fifty years ago Albizzi and Medici had been bitterly opposed: the Albizzi as heads of the oligarchy, the Medici of the popular party; they seemed to be taking up the same positions now. "Little is wanting to Cosimo," Rinaldo is supposed to have said, "but the actual sceptre of government; or rather he has the sceptre, but hides it under his cloak. . . . The people have chosen him as their advocate, and look upon him as a god. . . . The people are all Mediceans." When Albizzi was momentarily triumphant, he charged the Medici, in the accusations drawn up against them, with complicity in all the revolts and plots against the Government since 1378, and made Cosimo appear responsible for all.

Cosimo was also popular with the Grandi, with many of whom he had family connections. His immense wealth was still more the cause of his influence. His father had probably begun that policy of buying up adherents by pecuniary assistance, of which Cosimo made a regular system. In a city of merchants and financiers, the richest banker, who has the control of foreign markets, and who can influence the financial transactions of the whole known world, must necessarily be a person of great importance, and it was exactly this position which Cosimo held. He was not above employing direct bribery, but he could do much that was not direct bribery, by rendering the financial position of his fellow-citizens satisfactory or intolerable to them as he pleased. He secured the favour of the poor and of the Church, by no means an inconsiderable force, by his liberal almsgiving and ecclesiastical buildings and endowments. Besides all this, he possessed exactly those valuable characteristics which Rinaldo lacked. He was patient and could wait his opportunity, silent and able to appear not to notice an affront; a good, if cynical judge of character, a man who could both choose men and silently but thoroughly rule them. By aiming low, he always attained his mark, and could then afford to aim higher. His manner, if not expansive, was conciliatory; he was respected by his bitterest enemies; he could accommodate himself to any circumstances, and suit his conversation to any company, nor did he try to force an uncomfortably high standard upon his unwilling contemporaries.

He was supported by a little phalanx of men of much ability, yet all a little less scrupulous than himself: men whom he could employ in all sorts of dirty work without soiling his own fingers: his cousin Averardo, bold, cunning, cruel; Puccio Pucci, a member of the Minor Arts, who had greatly distinguished himself on the Dieci, sagacious, prudent, crafty; Martino Martini, and a host of lesser men. Many of the younger, ambitious politicians crowded to his party, in which there seemed more room for individual expansion than with Rinaldo, who must be everything himself, and could brook no rival. There were Alamanno Salviati, Agnolo Acciaiuoli, Dietisalvi Neroni, Luca Pitti, all of whose names were to become historical within the next few years. It was the interest of these lesser men to foster jealousy between their leaders in order to gain importance for themselves in the general struggle for power; the absence of Rinaldo and Cosimo from Florence for a great part of 1432, the former at Rome, the latter at Ferrara, gave opportunity for calumnious tongues.

Even in 1431 an inferior member of the party was hinting to Averardo that there were plots afoot against Cosimo: "you ought to tell Cosimo to speak the truth to those who try to take away his honour." Filelfo, the Greek scholar and teacher, and a bitter enemy of the Medici, was in correspondence with Milan, and was ready to propagate reports of a supposed intrigue between the Medici and Visconti.

The question of how long and how far Cosimo had been deliberately scheming to make himself master of the Republic, or whether he ever schemed for the position at all before it was thrust upon him, is a difficult one to answer. It was certainly not he and his friends who began the Lucchese war, but did they not deliberately try to prolong it in order to increase their own importance, and to seize upon the dissensions it caused as their opportunity? It was said that "because they had so much money they felt themselves to be rulers of everything in time of war"—"they made themselves great by keeping the war going, and by lending money to the Commune; which was safe and of great advantage to them, for to the people they appeared to be the supporters of the Commune; so that to them there accrued honour and power and position."

No doubt the Medici did make capital out of the circumstances of the war. The alliance with Rinaldo during its earlier months was profitable. Alamanno

Salviati wrote to Averardo that Rinaldo "is and has been a very useful man, though I may say to you that we do not love him much." Cosimo gained a reputation for great capabilities on the Dieci; Averardo was commissioned to secure the services of the Condottiere, Michele Sforza, and was afterwards Commissioner at his camp. And Cosimo certainly did come to the assistance of the Commune with large voluntary loans, which he could easily afford, and which enabled the Republic to tide over her financial difficulties. To Cosimo this was but another useful way of investing his wealth,— buying adherents wholesale instead of singly, in fact,— and while lesser men found their business seriously damaged by the heavy taxation, the Medici house could stand the strain with ease, and provide these loans into the bargain.

But there is no proof of the virulent assertions of their enemies that the Medici schemed to hinder the success of the siege of Lucca. Nor can it be proved that Lorenzo de' Medici, when Ambassador to Milan in 1430 to prevent the Duke from interfering in the war, was really engaged in secretly arranging Francesco Sforza's expedition to embarrass Florence and lengthen out hostilities. The charge that Averardo had a secret understanding first with Michele Sforza, and then with another general, Tolentino, has more verisimilitude. The same charge was made by Rinaldo against Neri Capponi with regard to Fortebraccio, and was later made against Rinaldo himself with regard to Piccinino. Certainly Averardo had urged that Michele Sforza should be taken into the Florentine service. He himself negotiated the affair with Michele, and was so long about it that suspicions of his honesty were aroused in Florence. Michele was an unsatisfactory soldier, and Averardo was Commissioner in his camp. The General's laziness and carelessness may have been paid for by the Commissioner in order that the war should be lengthened out; on the other hand, Averardo's failure to make Michele work may just as well have been due to incapacity, and, besides, what General did the Florentines ever find satisfactory? That Tolentino was in the pay of the Medici is certain, because of his action later on when Cosimo's life was in danger. It is possible in this case also that the paymasters deprecated excessive zeal on the part of the soldier in putting an end to the war; but there is no proof even here that Tolentino was paid for anything but to be useful to the Medici in case of need.

It cannot well be decided which party was responsible for the final outbreak of hostilities in 1433. Rinaldo struck the first blow, but we do not know how much provocation he may have received. The struggle had certainly been going on with more or less secrecy for some time,—each party scheming to get its members into the public offices, particularly into the Signory. Accusations were freely bandied about; there were plots and intrigues on all sides. There is a story that Rinaldo's warmest supporter, Niccolò Barbadori, had, quite two years previously, formed a plan for banishing Cosimo when he himself should be Gonfalonier, but that Niccolò Uzzano had dissuaded him. The story is rather improbable, since the rivalry between Rinaldo and Cosimo could then have been hardly in existence; yet it may be true that Uzzano tried to play them off against one another, and thus to recover his own predominance; so it is possible that he may have been responsible for the beginning of the enmity between them. Though but a few years before he had recommended a Parliament as a remedy for all the difficulties of the oligarchy, Uzzano seems by this time to have become averse to such a measure, if Barbadori really suggested it. "Whoever first makes a Parliament will be digging his own grave," are the words now put into his mouth by the chronicler. Probably he realised that what might a few years since have been a useful measure would be most risky now that the strength of the opposition was so much increased. But Uzzano's death left Rinaldo with a free hand, and Rinaldo was ready to risk anything against Cosimo. He seems to have been quite overwrought with excited jealousy: he who used to boast of his openness exclaimed angrily that he dared not speak even in private, because all that was said was repeated to the Signory.

In May, when his work on the Dieci was over, Cosimo retired to his country house in the Mugello, either to mature his plans or because, not feeling himself able to strike at his opponents, he really wished to escape them for a time. It is said that he was warned by a prophetic friar that his life would shortly be in danger. Perhaps he hoped that during his retirement Rinaldo's attention would be diverted elsewhere. In August, Alamanno Salviati wrote to Averardo at Pisa: "The magistrates are behaving as badly as, or worse than, ever, and I think we shall get no advantage, because of the ambition and pride" of Rinaldo. "Cosimo is very little here, and it seems to me not a good thing that the city should be abandoned by her citizens." Public excitement was not decreased by Cosimo's retirement; "everything that happened was made into a political question." The secrecy which was supposed to attend the appointment of the Signory was violated; every one could guess who would be the next Gonfalonier and Priors; speculation on their probable action much increased the general excitement. For the Signory of September and October, the Gonfalonier was almost certain to be Bernardo Guadagni, whose father had been Rinaldo's closest friend; most of the other members of the Signory would be of the same party. Rinaldo felt that his opportunity had come, and prepared to seize it. Guadagni was "a specchio," that is to say, he was behindhand in the payment of his taxes, and so would forfeit his right to hold office. Rinaldo paid the money which he owed to the Commune, and in return received from Bernardo a pledge to act under his directions.

The events of the next few days will best be described in Cosimo's own words, quoted from his diary. "When the new Signory was drawn, there began to be a rumour that during their rule there would be a revolution, and it was written to me in the Mugello, where I had been for some months in order to escape from the contests and divisions of the city, that I ought to return, and so I returned on September 4th. On the same day I visited the Gonfalonier and one of the Priors, whom I considered to be my friend, and who was under great obligations to me; and when I told them what was rumoured they immediately denied it, and told me to be of a good heart, for they hoped to leave the city at the end of their office in the same condition as they had found it. On the 5th they called a council of eight citizens, saying that they wished for their advice,"— amongst the eight were Rinaldo and Cosimo themselves,—"and although it was spread abroad about the town that a revolution was to be made, yet having had the assurances of the Signory, I did not credit the report. It followed that on the morning of the 7th, under colour of the said Council, they sent for me, and when I had arrived at the Palace I found the greater part of the company there; and, remaining there to deliberate, after some time I was commanded by the Signory to go upstairs, and by the Captain of the Infantry" (the Signorial bodyguard) "I was put into a room called the Barberia" (in the bell-tower of the Palace). Such underhand proceedings were indeed unlike the Rinaldo of former days!

"On hearing this all the city was moved," added Cosimo, and another writer of his party said that the people "were all terrified and did not know what to do." Amongst the lower classes "every one prayed with vows and tears that the Divine Justice would save him from a violent death." The Signory themselves seem to have been rather frightened at what they had done: some one going to the Palace found "arms everywhere; some ran upstairs, some down, some talked, some shouted; everything was full of passion, excitement, and fear." Rinaldo's son Ormanno and some other young members of his party filled the Piazza round the Palace with armed followers, to keep down the danger of a popular tumult, or to prevent any attempt to rescue Cosimo by force. The noise in the square beneath his prison must have been sufficiently alarming to the prisoner, who was not, like Rinaldo, inclined to make any display of personal courage. Indeed, we are told that he "fell down in a swoon" when his jailer entered his prison to announce his sentence. Until reassured on the word of honour of the jailer, who was rather favourable to him than otherwise, Cosimo refused to touch any food but a little bread, from fear of poison. His fear was probably not misplaced; obnoxious prisoners of whom it was difficult to get rid by legal means did not unfrequently die sudden and unexplained deaths in Italian prisons in the fifteenth century.

Had Cosimo resisted, refused to appear at the Palace, thrown himself upon his party and raised a popular revolution in the city, it is difficult to tell what the result would have been. He seems to have been afraid to run the risk, and when he was in prison his party were afraid to run it for him. The Signory had made an effort to capture Lorenzo, who was in Florence, and Averardo, who was at Pisa, but both escaped to the Mugello, where they collected a number of peasants who were attached to the Medici house; and on the day after Cosimo's imprisonment the Condottiere Tolentino, who was supposed to have a secret understanding with the Medici, marched his troops to within a few miles of the city, perhaps expecting to be encouraged to proceed by a rising there. Then, however, he or his employers lost heart. "They were counselled," Cosimo wrote, "not to raise a revolt, which might cause personal violence to be used against me." Tolentino withdrew therefore, making excuses to the Signory for moving without their orders. Averardo and Lorenzo, collecting all the portable valuables they could, left the Florentine dominions for Venice. "But," wrote Cosimo, "it was not a wise decision that they took; for had they gone forward I should have been set free, and he who was the cause of all would have been ruined." But Cosimo wrote this some time afterwards, when the personal danger was over.

Meanwhile the question of what to do with Cosimo now they had captured him remained to be settled by the captors. They had hoped at least to compass his financial ruin, but this hope was disappointed; Cosimo's connections were too widely extended without Florence, for his business to be so easily ruined. "For we," he himself wrote, "did not lose credit, but great sums of money were offered to us by many foreign merchants and princes." Some of his more violent enemies wished him to be murdered in prison; but the majority at least desired everything to be done in constitutional form.

Immediately after his seizure, the Signory, as they had the power to do, banished Cosimo, his brother, and Averardo, for five years each. Then, because it was felt that such a very moderate punishment of its leaders was not sufficient to crush their party, and in order to gain, at least nominally, the popular sanction for more stringent measures, a Parliament was held in the square of the Palace on September 9th. The great bell of the Palace was rung, the approaches to the square were guarded by Ormanno degli Albizzi and his armed followers, such citizens as could be got together —Cosimo said that there were only twenty-three, and he may have been able to count from the window of his prison—were assembled in the square, and shouted lustily "Si! Si!" (Yes! Yes!) to the proposals made by the Chancellor of the Signory from the Ringhiera. Balìa was given to a Committee of over two hundred persons, including, of course, all the leading members of the Albizzi party, and also, in order to give an appearance of impartiality, a certain number of people who were thought to be compliant. Amongst the names of the members we find those of Palla Strozzi, Niccolò Barbadori, and Ridolfo Peruzzi, Rinaldo's most active partisan, but neither Lorenzo Ridolfi nor Agnolo Pandolfini, who both disapproved of these violent measures.

The first duty of the Balìa was to decide on Cosimo's fate, and then the radical weakness of the party at once manifested itself. Some of the members of the Balìa, says Machiavelli, "urged Cosimo's death, some his exile, some were silent, either out of compassion for him or out of fear" for themselves. Another measure, we learn, could not be passed for some hours, and then only by the pertinacity of the Signory. So difficult was it even to get the members to attend meetings of the Balìa, that a provision was made by which two-thirds of those present, instead of two-thirds of the whole number, constituted a legal majority. At first the Balìa would only pass short sentences of banishment on the Medici; these were afterwards extended to ten years, but no more could be obtained against them, although Cosimo was kept in prison on purpose to frighten his friends by threats against his life.

The fact was that, as usual, the oligarchs could not cling together. The Gonfalonier himself, pledged as he was to Rinaldo, was now intriguing in Cosimo's favour. For, as soon as Cosimo, through the kindly help of his jailer, obtained communications with the outer world, he fell back upon his family policy. The Gonfalonier was bribed with a thousand florins, and another member of the Signory with a less sum. Cosimo thought his personal safety cheap at the price. "They had little spirit," he said, "for if they had wanted money, they should have had ten thousand or more to deliver me from that peril." Not without effect either was the pleading in his favour of ambassadors from Venice, where the Medici banking firm was held in high repute, and it was felt that its loss of credit would cause a wide-spread dislocation of finance. In Venice, at least, the charge against Cosimo of intriguing with Milan cannot have been believed.

At length, on October 3rd, after four weeks' imprisonment, Cosimo was liberated, and sent to the frontier under safe escort,—the Signory being quite ready to protect him from assassination. His journey was a small triumph in itself. The Contadini (country people), with whom the Medici were always very popular, crowded to meet him and give him presents, more as if he were an ambassador than a fallen politician going into banishment. The place of exile assigned to him being Padua, the Marquess of Ferrara sent an escort to conduct him safely through his territories; in the Venetian dominions he met with equal honour. Venice petitioned the Signory of Florence that he might be allowed to reside anywhere within her territories, and the Signory were again complaisant. Cosimo went to live in Venice itself, which was already his brother's place of exile. Honours were showered upon him; he was treated exactly as if he were a Florentine ambassador. He himself wrote, "It would hardly be believed that, having been driven from my home, I should find so much honour." Lorenzo's son wrote to his cousin, the son of Averardo, "It would not be possible to describe the condolences made every day at our house . . . the love which these Venetians bear to Cosimo they have shown by their deeds." In Venice it was foreseen that Cosimo's exile could not last long: perhaps it was guessed how soon he would be master of Florence, director of Florentine politics, and a valuable ally. Perhaps, too, the Venetians suspected that Albizzi would not remain faithful to their anti-Milanese League.

Cosimo lived quietly at Venice, seeming to attend only to his business, and to the building of a library as a kind of thank-offering to his hosts; he was content to let the Albizzi party "fill up the cup," and complete their ruin by their own mistakes. We even find that he and Lorenzo furnished the Signory with some "valuable information," for which they were duly thanked. But he was not without communications with those of his party who remained in Florence, and kept him posted in all that was passing there.

As was only to be expected, Cosimo's banishment did not in the least improve the state of affairs in Florence. It caused much discontent amongst the lower classes, who felt that they had lost a real benefactor. They lamented "the banishment of so glorious a citizen as was Cosimo, the pillar, fountain, and banner of all Italy, and the father of the poor." No doubt, too, the commercial inconvenience of the absence of all the Medici from Florence was found very great; and such heads of business firms as were not devoted to the Albizzi were eager to have them back. Fresh military expenses in the following year made the Republic feel the want of Cosimo's purse, ever open to supply her needs. The Moderates, Agnolo Pandolfini and Palla Strozzi for example, disapproved strongly of what had been done; and though Palla gave his countenance to the Government, he opposed much of Rinaldo's policy.

"The city remained as if stunned," said one contemporary; and Machiavelli wrote, "Florence, remaining widowed of a citizen so universally loved, every one was confounded, both the conquered and the conquerors." For now that their chief danger was apparently removed, the triumphant oligarchs continued to prosecute their private ambitions and enmities, most of them without a thought that the banishment of Cosimo did not involve the extinction of his party. Rinaldo knew better; he realised that "either a great man should not be touched at all, or, if he is touched, should be crushed utterly"; but Rinaldo was almost powerless. The jealousy which had lately been directed upon Cosimo was now turned against himself; his own followers feared that he would become too powerful, now that he had no great rival. His honest refusal to permit the suspension of the Catasto no doubt added to his unpopularity with them. The Government, from September 1433 to September 1434, was accordingly distinguished by its futility, incapacity, and uncertainty. Cosimo's literary friend, Niccolò de' Niccoli, dared in public to send him a message that "so many errors are made every day by this Government that a folio of paper would not be sufficient to contain them all."

Rinaldo's first attempts to rule were made through the Balìa. With much difficulty he persuaded it to grant new and important powers to the Police Magistracy, called the "Otto di Balìa," so that it might prevent any attempts at a counter-revolution. But the most important point to secure was the control of the election of the Signory, for if a Signory, the majority of whose members were favourable to Cosimo, should obtain office, a new struggle must certainly take place. Here Rinaldo was hampered by his own scruples. Afraid of in any way infringing the Constitution, he had only allowed the Balìa the power to add new names to the Borse from which the Signory were drawn, and the old names still remained in them. There was no danger in this so long as each Signory, instead of being drawn by lot, was selected from the Borse by a carefully-chosen committee of the Balìa, called the Accopiatori; but Rinaldo seems to have been so anxious to govern constitutionally that the power of the Accopiatori was limited in duration, and was to expire within a year, when the Signory would again be drawn by lot. This may have been justice, but it was none the less dangerous. Rinaldo never quite realised that the chief object of a party trying to rule Florence should be to get the official government entirely under its control. There was much complaint, both now and always, that "the citizens were more powerful than the laws." Rinaldo, in trying to act according to the Constitution and obey the laws, forgot that in so doing he was freeing the official government from its dependence upon his party, a partial freedom of which the official government made use before long to destroy the domination of his party altogether.

Rinaldo tried to lessen the danger by other means. A further proscription of Cosimo's party was attempted: the less important Medici were banished, then Puccio Pucci and Puccio's brother Giovanni, and lastly Agnolo Acciaiuoli, whose crime, according to Cosimo, was merely "certain information he had written to Puccio and to me, which was not of any great importance." According to his accusers he had advised Cosimo to do the very two things that they were most afraid he would do: stir up a foreign war, so that Florence might feel the want of his liberality, and make overtures of friendship to Neri Capponi.

Neri's attitude at the time of Cosimo's banishment seemed neutral; but, since just then the Signory ordered him to return to his official duties at Pisa, he was possibly distrusted already. In the spring of 1434, he, together with Alamanno Salviati and some other Mediceans, were accused of a plot to obtain Tolentino's services with the help of Venice, and secure Cosimo's restoration by force. Afterwards the Mediceans declared that this scheme had no real existence, and that it was invented by their enemies as a device to ruin those accused of it; but it does not seem intrinsically impossible that such a plan should have been contemplated by the friends of the exiles. In May a Signory, little attached to Rinaldo, went so far as to threaten to hold a new parliament and make another revolution, and were hardly deterred by the persuasions of Palla Strozzi, who was now trying to act the part of mediator.

Rinaldo's most statesmanlike scheme for securing the supremacy of his party was his proposed alliance with the Grandi, to whom he wished to open all the offices of the Republic, thus giving them the status of full citizenship. But the scheme only called forth angry assertions that "liberty and free government" would be endangered by giving political power to the Grandi,—a maxim which was true enough in the fourteenth century, but which should have been quite exploded by this time, since the Grandi had long ago ceased to be powerful enough to be dangerous. Some small concessions which Rinaldo procured did not conciliate them, and helped to alienate his own supporters.

Rinaldo was almost desperate. We find him speaking in the Pratiche in language strangely humble and unlike his former self, entreating instead of commanding. The weakness of his position appears in the imposition of a new "Oath of Unity" upon all the leading citizens,—an oath taken, indeed, but never kept. He seems to have turned in despair to foreign politics, hoping through them to strengthen himself at home. Pope Eugenius IV., driven from Rome by Visconti's threatening Condottieri without and discontented citizens within, was offered an asylum in Florence, which he gladly accepted. Rinaldo hoped that the Pope's gratitude might make him a powerful ally, but at the same time he was playing a double game, and negotiating secretly with Visconti, the Pope's enemy, and with Visconti's chief Condottiere, Piccinino. We cannot ascertain the precise extent of this intrigue, into which Rinaldo was probably driven by the favour shown to Cosimo by Venice; but certainly, when Rinaldo himself became an exile, he retired at once to Milan, as if he counted on finding help there. For the present the intrigue only alienated the Pope, since he found Rinaldo unwilling to let Florentine troops join his own to withstand Visconti's new attacks on Romagna. Rinaldo was, however, overruled; the troops were sent, and in August suffered a heavy defeat, which only served to increase the unpopularity of the Government.

And just as the news of this defeat was upsetting the Florentines, another event threw all parties into a turmoil. The power of Rinaldo's Accopiatori came to an end, and the selection of the Signory was again by lot. The very first Signory thus drawn, that of September and October 1434, was found to include the names of several persons openly favourable to Cosimo, amongst them Niccolò Donati, the Gonfalonier. A few days elapsed between the drawing of the Signory and its entrance into office. Rinaldo and his more energetic followers were anxious to seize this brief opportunity of striking the first blow and averting the threatened danger. It was proposed that the Signory still sitting should, before their term of office expired, hold another Parliament, obtain a new Balìa, which should elect another Signory to take the place of that which had just been drawn by lot, and banish a number of the opponents of the Government. But this plan had to be abandoned mainly on account of the opposition of Palla Strozzi, who maintained that the new Signory would not attempt to raise a revolution within the city while external affairs were in so critical a condition.

It was therefore decided to wait and see what the Signory would do. Soon after coming into office, they showed their intentions by the trial and condemnation of the last Gonfalonier, a follower of Rinaldo, for peculation. Then it was discovered that arms were being collected in the Palace, and preparations made for a struggle. A message was sent to Cosimo, bidding him start for Florence; "offering, when they should hear that I was near, to restore me to the city," wrote Cosimo himself. It was obvious that Rinaldo must resort to force if he wished to avert the coming revolution; and, as success in these urban contests usually lay with those who struck the first blow, Rinaldo and his most active adherents, Ridolfo Peruzzi and Niccolò Barbadori, planned to seize the Palace by a surprise attack on September 25th, to make the Signory prisoners, then to raise the lower classes and employ them in the congenial amusement of house-burning,—the houses of the Medici, Alamanno Salviati, and others were to suffer,—while the revolution was being accomplished at the Palace. The plot was discovered by the Signory, it is said through the means of Neri Capponi; preparations were made to resist the attack on the Palace; food, arms, and soldiers collected within it, and the attempt was frustrated. On the following day, September 26th, Rinaldo called a meeting of his party in arms on the large Piazza of S. Apollinare, in the rear of the Palace, intending, as soon as troops of peasants which he had been raising in the country districts should arrive, to march from thence to the Piazza of the Signoria, and so surround the Palace on all sides. Peruzzi, Barbadori, and many others came, and there was, of course, a crowd of loafers and soldiers out of employment, "whose noses were longer than their honesty," says the chronicler, and who were willing to destroy and burn anything in the hopes of plunder. But of the respectable lower and middle class citizens there were none. Their sympathies were with Cosimo, but they disliked fighting and disturbances too much to take up arms on either side, so they merely closed their shops and shut themselves up at home. Still more serious for Rinaldo was the defection of some greater men on whom he had counted. Palla Strozzi is said to have appeared, but unarmed; and, when Rinaldo rebuked his slackness, to have returned home and taken no further part in the revolution. Palla's defection decided many waverers to follow his example.

The Signory, much frightened at the collection of some eight hundred armed men close to the Palace, despatched a messenger to some troops in Florentine pay, who were not far from the city, with orders to march to their aid. Rinaldo sent a counter-message bidding them stay where they were, but the revolution was all over before they could have arrived. Meanwhile, the Signory called upon all loyal citizens to defend the legal magistracy against armed rebellion. Rinaldo had in fact put himself technically in the wrong by taking up arms, and besides the regular Mediceans, Pitti, Alessandri, Martelli, and so forth, many moderate people, not greatly attached to Cosimo, obeyed the call of the Signory on these grounds.

Then, feeling themselves strong enough to treat, the Signory sent three citizens, reputed neutrals, to the Piazza of S. Apollinare, promising that if all there would lay down arms there should be no revolution, and Cosimo should not be recalled. Ridolfo Peruzzi, already losing heart, professed to be satisfied, and proceeded to the Palace, where he met with an honourable reception. Rinaldo found his following melting away, while the Signory grew stronger every minute. The reinforcements which he had expected from the country did not arrive; perhaps he had counted on help from Piccinino, but no help came.

At this critical moment, when bloodshed was impending, the Pope, who was still staying in Florence at the Convent of Sᵃ Maria Novella, took up the rôle of mediator. In spite of accusations made against him, there is no doubt that he meant to act quite honestly. Florence was his principal mainstay and ally, and a bloody revolution within Florence would fatally weaken her energies for external warfare. It was Rinaldo who had brought him to Florence, but Rinaldo was acting the part of a rebel to his own government. Probably Eugenius hoped that his mediation might save Rinaldo from the worst consequences of rebellion. At the same time he could not but feel that, if Cosimo were restored and made the director of Florentine policy, the alliance with himself and Venice, from which Rinaldo was departing, would be confirmed and fortified. He accordingly sent Vitelleschi, the militant Bishop of Recanati, afterwards Archbishop of Florence and a Cardinal and Patriarch, and, as Cosimo said, "very much my friend," to try mediation. Vitelleschi went backwards and forwards between the Signory and Rinaldo, and at last, about five o'clock in the evening, persuaded the latter to leave S. Apollinare and go to have an interview with the Pope himself at Sᵃ Maria Novella. Accompanied by all his followers, Rinaldo repaired thither, and "the last of them had not left the Piazza when the first reached the Convent." Rinaldo and some of the chief of the party went within to discuss affairs with the Pope. It may not be true that, as a very anti-

Papal chronicler put it, "the infinite tears of the Pope issued from the same source as those of the crocodile," but at least Eugenius succeeded in making Rinaldo, already discouraged by the defection of his party, believe that he could arrange matters for him with the Signory, and secure their pardon for the revolt. Meanwhile, the crowd without grew weary of waiting; a rumour arose that there was to be no fighting; finally, all dispersed without further disturbance. The revolution was practically over.

Rinaldo remained with the Pope that night for safety, but within a day or two it was obvious how utterly he had failed. The Signory called in troops from all parts to keep order in the town; Neri Capponi and others, who had hitherto held aloof to see what would happen, hastened to give in their adherence. On the 29th the Piazza was well guarded with troops, and a Parliament was held. Balìa was given to three hundred and fifty persons, including all the Medici party, and many moderate men like Palla Strozzi. Their powers were almost unlimited; and their first action was, of course, to decree, by an overwhelming majority, the recall of the exiles, Medici, Pucci, and Agnolo Acciaiuoli. A day or two later sentences of banishment were passed against Rinaldo degli Albizzi and his son Ormanno; and similar sentences upon Ridolfo Peruzzi, Niccolò Barbadori and others soon followed.

Had it not been for the Pope's mediation, Rinaldo might have had to pay the penalty with his life, but beyond this Eugenius was powerless to protect him. It was impossible that Cosimo and he should remain together in the same city. Nor does the Pope appear to have disapproved of the course that things had taken; Vitelleschi and other ecclesiastical dignitaries supported the Signory on the balcony of the Palace at the Parliament; two days later the Signory themselves repaired to Sᵃ Maria Novella to thank the Pope for the part which he had played, and on his return Cosimo did the same. Certainly it was due to Eugenius that an inevitable revolution was accomplished without bloodshed.

Rinaldo must have left the Florentine territory almost on the same day that his triumphant rival re-entered it. In accordance with the summons of the Signory, Cosimo and Lorenzo left Venice, Averardo remaining behind there ill, and when they reached the Ferrarese territory they received news from Florence of the events of September 26th and 29th, and a pressing invitation to hasten homewards. To quote Cosimo himself: "On October 5th, exactly at the end of a year, on the same day and in the same hour, we re-entered the territory of the Commune, and at the same place. Which I have recorded because it was said to us by many devoted and good persons when we were exiled that a year would not pass before we should be restored and return to Florence." Once within the territory, the exiles found great companies of friends and followers assembled to meet and congratulate them. Florence was entered late in the evening, and by a circuitous route, in order to avoid the crowds waiting in the street between the gate and the Medici house. The Medici visited the Signory to thank them for their good offices, and remained with them all that night, "lest a disturbance should be made"; but, no doubt, when next day they rode from the Palace to their house in the Via Larga, the Florentines were able to shout and cheer to their heart's content. The Medici had become immensely popular, and the crowd must have enjoyed making a noise over their return.

Once in power, the Medicean party were not going to fall into Rinaldo's most obvious mistake, that of not making the proscription of their rivals sufficiently sweeping. "The vengeance," said a contemporary chronicler, "is always greater than the first offence; and for the sake of one family twenty were driven from Florence." In the Pratiche Cosimo himself and Neri Capponi urged clemency, and advised that only the heads should be punished, and the rank and file allowed to go free; but Cosimo's partisans were too full of their triumph to be satisfied by half measures, and Cosimo either could not, or did not try to, control them. Punishment in one form or another fell upon some hundreds of persons, the crime of many of whom was merely that they belonged to families whom it was desirable to suppress. According to the fullest reckoning, about eighty persons were banished for longer or shorter terms, a great number were made Grandi, that is, permanently disenfranchised, others were declared incapable of holding office for a term of years. Eleven whole families, including the Albizzi and Peruzzi, were completely cut off from the government, their descendants yet unborn being included in the proscription. Amongst others upon whom punishment fell very hardly was Palla Strozzi, who, in attempting to moderate both parties, succeeded in pleasing neither. He was one of the newly appointed Balìa, and seemed to have no cause for uneasiness. He had thought himself the "particular friend" of Cosimo, had once received financial assistance from him, and had tried to prevent his banishment. But he had been too distinguished a member of the late government to be passed over by the new; his very presence in Florence "seemed a reproach to them," and he was banished for ten years together with the heads of the Albizzi party. The proscriptions continued till the end of the year. In January Cosimo himself was Gonfalonier, and he skilfully contrived that there should be a cessation of condemnations for the two months during which he held office, and that some exiles, who had broken their bounds, been declared rebels, captured, and brought back to Florence, should be condemned to perpetual imprisonment instead of death. But in March there were fresh condemnations, and some real and supposed plots against the Government were sternly suppressed. Cosimo's apologists declare that he regretted all this severity, but was unable to prevent it, or to control those more violent members of his party to whom he owed his restoration, and who thought that the least reward that he could give them was freedom to gratify all their personal enmities. But it is doubtful whether Cosimo exerted himself very much to control them; and in the long run they had the odium and he the advantage of their severe measures.

Thus, after more than half a century of power, fell the "Ottimati," the aristocrats, who had ruled Florence ever since the suppression of the Ciompi revolt. For the last fifteen years their power had been on the wane. Success had caused internal disunion, disunion had caused failures, above all the failure of the Lucchese war, and failure had still further divided the already broken ranks of the ruling party. While factions in the Government were struggling amongst themselves for the possession of supreme power, room had been left for the growth of new forces and the revival of old, but still more for the rise of new men,—men who had either no hereditary share in the government, or who, like the Medici themselves, thought that there was more chance of gratifying their ambitions by alliance with the discontented classes,—by a virtual "leadership of the opposition."

For there was not much apparent difference in principle between the Governments before and after 1434, there was rather a difference of persons, or, more precisely, of families. The supreme power still seemed to be in the hands of a clique of powerful houses; yet there were two distinctions, which after all were not far from fundamental. The dictatorship of the Medici themselves over their own party was much more complete than that of the Albizzi had been; it extended further into every department, not only of political, but of social, life in Florence. Secondly, and the second distinction was a result of the first, the ranks of the governing party were much less narrow; to enter them it was only necessary to please the Medici, and the strength of the Medici enabled them to admit new men with far greater freedom and safety than the oligarchy had been able to do.

It was this very narrowness, inherent to its character as an oligarchy, that led to one of the chief causes of the fall of the last Government. In self-preservation unable to admit new men and new families to its ranks, it had been equally unable to admit new wealth. The balance of wealth had in fact shifted; and that political power follows wealth is an elementary maxim in all politics,—a maxim which is particularly true of commercial states like Florence, where the possession of wealth and social power went literally hand in hand. It was no longer the Albizzi and the Strozzi who were the "millionaires" of Florence; it was the Medici, and after them such new families as the Pitti and the Pucci, the latter still only members of the Minor Arts. These men forced themselves into prominence, and formed a party numerically and physically more powerful than the ruling party itself.

But the control of the official government was the point on which the Albizzi finally fell. At the last moment they had made an effort to recover their power, in substituting the election of the Signory by Accopiatori appointed by themselves for its selection by lot. But their use of the Parliament and Balìa for this purpose, as Uzzano had so long ago advised, was, in 1433, some years too late. The opposition,—the Mediceans and their allies,—wrested the official government out of their hands, made use of the great theoretical powers of the Signory to crush that very party which had so long used those powers for its own purposes, and substituted themselves in its place.

CHAPTER III

FOREIGN POLICY FROM 1435 TO 1447—THE VENETIAN ALLIANCE—THE BALANCE OF POWER

DURING the first few years after Cosimo's return from exile, the place which he took in the foreign policy of Florence was of comparatively secondary importance. His energies were employed in securing his position at home, and he had not yet obtained that hold upon the political and diplomatic machinery of the Commune which afterwards enabled him to make the Florentines bend their inclinations to his will. He also found Florence already committed to a particular foreign policy, which had been shaped by circumstances not in her own control, and from the force of which he too could not escape. Since it was a policy of circumstances, and not of design, it is very difficult to judge how far he was instrumental in controlling its details. His name appears very seldom; and when he does act in person, it is rather as the exponent of the national, than as the initiator of an original, foreign policy. In such independent action as was possible to him, he could be nothing more than opportunist; he could do no more than make the best of certain chances which came in his way. During these early years, however, those political conditions, and those ideas and aims of his own were gradually formed, which in after years determined his independent foreign policy.

Florence at this time, it has been said, was guided by necessity. Filippo Maria Visconti, Duke of Milan, greedy, shifty and faithless, was endangering by his intrigues and ambition the neighbouring Powers,—Venice, Florence, and the Pope,—who were forced to hold together in order to withstand him. Florence had no great love for Venice, her commercial rival; yet however cavalierly Venice might treat her, she was obliged to cling to the Venetian Alliance. In Naples, the war between the rival claimants to the throne, Alfonso, King of Aragon, and René, Duke of Anjou, was just beginning; Florence, which had an old and sincere affection for the Angevin House, favoured René. The alliance of Alfonso and Visconti, which was formed soon after Cosimo's return from exile, was directed therefore both against the Angevins in Naples, and against the League of the two Republics and the Pope in the north. Thus Italy was divided into two rival and fairly equal camps.

During the past few months Cosimo had identified himself personally with the anti-Milanese attitude of Florence. The kind reception that he had met with at Venice, and the personal friendships that he had formed there, bound him to the policy of the Venetian League. Pope Eugenius had assisted in restoring him to Florence in order that he might counteract Albizzi's growing tendency to desert the League and join Visconti. Immediately on their banishment the Albizzi and some other exiles, leaving the localities to which they had been ordered, took refuge in Milan, and attempted to stir up Visconti to invade Tuscany, promising him that a revolution in their favour would take place in Florence immediately on their approach, if they were backed by an armed force.

The first necessity for the League was to find a general, since Cosimo's friend Tolentino had been taken prisoner, and, by Visconti's order, murdered. For this purpose Francesco Sforza, in whose military capabilities the League had unbounded faith, seemed the most suitable person. Sforza's hands were indeed tied by his betrothal to Bianca Visconti, Filippo's illegitimate daughter, whose hand and the possible reversion of Milan Sforza was so anxious to obtain that he always hesitated to act freely against her father. Yet since Visconti was continually intriguing against his future son-in-law, of whom he was both jealous and afraid, and attempting to deprive him of the property which he held in the district of the March, it seemed possible, by working on Sforza's distrust of Visconti, and his constant need of money for the maintenance of his estates and his army, to make him a useful servant to the League.

Another difficulty in the employment of Sforza lay in the great importance of retaining the Pope as a member of the League, since an alliance between him and Visconti would lead to an unlimited extension of Milanese influence in Romagna. Eugenius seemed to be bound to the League by Visconti's adoption of the cause of Alfonso of Aragon at Naples, since the Pope favoured the Angevins; but at the same time Eugenius could never peacefully acquiesce in Sforza's retention of the March, which was Church property, and it was therefore one of the chief tasks of the League to keep the peace between them. Just after Cosimo's return from exile, Sforza succeeded in clearing the rest of the Papal states from Visconti's Condottieri, whom he permitted, and secretly prompted, to carve out estates for themselves there as they pleased. In the winter of 1435-36 Sforza visited Florence to receive the thanks of the Pope in person; he was received with great enthusiasm in the city, where at this time he was very popular, partly on account of the Tuscan origin of his mother and his own early bringing up in Tuscany. This visit had a result of the utmost importance, which largely shaped the history of Italy for the next half century. Sforza and Cosimo met for the first time since the latter had become ruler of Florence, and a close friendship was formed between them, which lasted all their lives and was bequeathed to their immediate descendants. From this time Sforza always wrote to Cosimo as to his "father"; he declared that Cosimo's interests "are identical with my own, his wishes are mine."

Sforza saw that, if he was to acquire Milan in the future, he could not do better than make a firm ally of a man in whom he could already discern the great political and diplomatic abilities which Cosimo afterwards displayed, and who seemed to the needy, spendthrift Condottiere a perfect mine of wealth. Cosimo, his whole mind bent on securing his own position in Florence, considered that a soldier of Sforza's powers, devoted to his service personally, and to that of the Republic when necessary, might prove a valuable ally.

Accordingly when, in 1436, Florence was threatened with war, Sforza was immediately called to her defence.

The ostensible cause of the war was the aid sent by the two Republics to Genoa, which had rebelled against Visconti. The real cause was Visconti's hope of making use of the Florentine exiles to attack and embarrass Florence, and to weaken her by prolonging her internal discords; perhaps, too, he believed that the exiles on their restoration would make Florence abandon the Venetian Alliance. Rinaldo wrote to Cosimo, "The hen is sitting"; but Cosimo, well aware that threats of an armed invasion were more likely to alienate than to conciliate the Florentines, retorted with his customary coolness, "She will find it hard to sit outside the nest."

Twice during 1436 Ormanno degli Albizzi accompanied expeditions to Lucca, threatening Florence from thence. On the second occasion, the captain of the invading force was the famous Condottiere, Piccinino, who had given Florence so much trouble in the late Lucchese war. Sforza was summoned to oppose him, and as soon as he arrived the idea occurred to the Florentines that now, with the best general in Italy at their service, was the opportunity for a fresh attempt to conquer Lucca. It was, in fact, of the utmost importance to the Mediceans that the acquisition of Pisa by the Albizzi should be balanced by another conquest under their *régime*,—the conquest, in fact, of that very town which the Albizzi had so lately failed to secure. The attack upon Lucca which they accordingly undertook was immensely popular in Florence; all parties united in their desire for conquest; many private persons lent money voluntarily to the Dieci. When after all the attempt failed, the disappointment was bitter; indeed, as Machiavelli afterwards observed, "no one who had lost his own property could have been more indignant than were the Florentines at failing to secure the property of others."

The causes of the failure were two: the unwilling half-heartedness of Sforza, and the selfish greediness of Venice. Sforza did not wish to alienate Visconti irrevocably; he was therefore from the first slow and laggard in the conduct of the war; he would not do anything at all except when forced either by the exhortations of the Florentine commissioner, Neri Capponi, and by letters from Cosimo; or by very shame at allowing Piccinino to carry off all the honours. He was willing to please his soldiers by letting them lay waste the country round Lucca in time-honoured fashion, and he conquered with ease a number of the fortresses; but he made no attempt to push on the siege of Lucca itself, until he found it convenient to do so as an excuse for not moving elsewhere.

For Venice, pressed hard by Visconti, and jealous of the possible acquisition of Lucca by Florence, suddenly laid claim to Sforza's services for herself. So far, as Florence justly complained, Venice had derived all the advantage from their common league; it seemed only fair that Florence should have her turn, and add Lucca to her dominions. But Venice preferred to keep Florence dependent on herself, and not to allow her to become equal to her, and therefore independent. Unluckily for Florence, Venice had the power of the purse, and refused to pay her share in Sforza's subsidy unless he obeyed her summons; "the Republic does not pay those who will not serve her," he was told. Sforza meanwhile had flatly refused to go; he was not bound by the terms of his service to fight north of the Po; Visconti was again bribing him with offers of his daughter, and Sforza had no intention of alienating him by attacking him in his own dominions. His excuse was that he was bound to the service of Florence by ties of honour and gratitude, and he began accordingly to press on the siege of Lucca. At the same time he told the Florentines that, if Venice refused his stipend, he could not remain in their service alone; he would need more support, must "seek other shoulders," come to an understanding, in fact, with Visconti. Cosimo, believing himself not without reason to be a *persona grata* in Venice since his residence there during his exile, had himself appointed ambassador, with the view of persuading her to give up her claims on Sforza, lest Sforza should really go over to Visconti and Florence should in self-defence be obliged to make peace. He met with a refusal, which at first was at least polite; "we are not jealous of your acquiring Lucca," he was told, "but we do not intend to pay the expenses of its conquest." This was particularly hard, since Florence had, in the last war, shared the expense of the capture of Bergamo and Brescia for Venice. Then Cosimo visited the Pope at Ferrara, and tried to persuade him to remove the Council for Union with the Greek Church, which he was holding at Ferrara, to Florence. The Albizzi had had their Council at Pisa; he also wished for the éclat and profit of entertaining the heads of the Church. His reception at Venice after his return from

Ferrara was even less cordial than before: "You," the Venetians said, no longer trying to hide their jealousy, "want to have the Council, you the Pope, you Lucca, you everything!" This suspicion indeed was common to both parties; Florence believed that Venice intended to acquire the empire of all Italy, and was firmly convinced that she was exhorting Lucca to hold out against Sforza.

The result of the attitude of Venice was what Cosimo had pointed out. Sforza went over to Visconti, and his betrothal to Bianca was renewed; Florence, left without a general, was obliged to accept Sforza's mediation between herself and Lucca. All that she acquired by the treaty which he arranged were three Lucchese fortresses, but the consequences of the war reached much further. For this was the first indication of that breach between Florence and Venice, which slowly but surely widened during the next twelve years, and at length converted the allies into the leaders of rival leagues. Cosimo, especially, never forgot the personal slight put upon him during his embassy, and it was the first step towards the conversion of his friendship for Venice into a deadly and persistent enmity.

It seemed that Florence was to have her opportunity for revenge on Venice almost immediately. Visconti, with Florence and Sforza neutral, was able to turn all his energies against Venice, which very shortly was in serious straits. She had no general worthy to oppose Piccinino, who was besieging Brescia and had cut off from it all possibilities of relief; she became almost desperate of preserving her mainland territory; "her state stands as if in water up to the throat, and is almost ruined," wrote

Sforza; and again, "the troops of Venice are as if they were not, so little do the Milanese esteem them." Venice was driven in her distress to send Jacopo Donato, Cosimo's host in exile, to ask aid from Florence, which she had so lately slighted. There was a natural inclination in Florence to leave her to her fate, and let her suffer the full effects of her conduct of the previous year. Cosimo, however, saw that to allow Visconti to crush Venice at his leisure was very far from a wise policy, and he persuaded the Signory to open fresh negotiations with Sforza. Sforza hesitated and shifted for some time; he still did not wish to fight north of the Po; he still had hopes of the conclusion of his marriage; but at last he gave way to the assurances of Neri Capponi that Visconti only meant to hold him in check by his promises of Bianca, while he conquered Venice unhindered. He took service once more under the League, and Neri went to Venice to arrange for his march thither. Neri was received with a show of gratitude very different from the reception accorded to Cosimo the year before; "their sorrow was turned into joy," Neri wrote; "they" (the Senate) "threw aside their black gowns, and gave themselves up to joy and feasting. Their funds," added the business-like Florentine, "rose several per cent."

Sforza's campaign in Lombardy in the year 1439 was very successful, and Venice hoped in the following year to recover all she had lost; but, early in 1440, Piccinino suddenly quitted Lombardy, and marched southwards towards Tuscany. Rinaldo degli Albizzi himself and other exiles were with him. With his usual bravado Rinaldo wrote to Cosimo that he "was not sleeping." "Probably not," Cosimo retorted, "since I have deprived you of sleep." Rinaldo and Piccinino had another ally in the Patriarch Vitelleschi, who was in command of the Papal forces. In 1434 he had been Cosimo's friend, and had done much to procure his restoration from exile; but he seems to have been prompted to change his party by jealousy of the influence which Cosimo exercised over the Pope, since Eugenius had, at Cosimo's request, moved the Council from Ferrara to Florence. Fortunately for Florence, the Pope was persuaded to believe in Vitelleschi's treachery, and Luca Pitti was despatched to Rome, and there carried through a somewhat shady plot, by which Vitelleschi was captured, and, whether by Pitti himself or not, was violently done to death. The Papal troops under Vitelleschi's successor were brought into Tuscany to supplement those with which Florence was preparing to face Piccinino.

Visconti had hoped by Piccinino's movement to manœuvre Sforza out of Lombardy, but Sforza had nevertheless remained where he was. Cosimo, who believed that Florence could defend herself without him, had advised him not to come to Tuscany as he wished. It was a great risk to run for Florence, and more particularly for Cosimo, lest, from fear of Piccinino, the city should consent to receive back the exiles; and indeed, when it was heard that Piccinino had forced his way over the mountains, had marched southwards by the Mugello route, and, crossing the Fiesole Hills, was passing over the Arno between Florence and the Pisan district, there was no little panic in the city, and for a time the stability of the Medici rule was tried to the uttermost. Had Piccinino remained on the Arno, and cut off the food supplies which Florence was accustomed to receive from Pisa, scarcity in the city and consequent discontent might really have produced a revolution. But Cosimo took the risk rather than break with Venice again by calling Sforza away. He understood, indeed, that Florence would suffer much rather than receive back the exiles by force, and run the risk of admitting a foreign army within her walls.

But Piccinino threw away his opportunities, and marched off into the Casentino, where Rinaldo had received offers of aid from an old friend, the Count of Poppi, head of the ancient Guidi family, which had been for many years "ricommandato" to Florence. Piccinino spent many weeks in reducing mountain fortresses in an out-of-the-way corner of Tuscany,—one little castle, S. Niccolò, holding out a full month,—while so great was the difficulty of procuring provisions in that barren country that, declaring that his horses "did not eat stones," he at length marched off his troops to his native city, Perugia, in the hope of carving out a principality for himself in that district. There he received letters from Visconti recalling him to Lombardy, where Sforza, unchecked, had been carrying on a completely successful campaign. Piccinino, feeling that his own presence in Lombardy was essential, started to obey, but the persuasions of the exiles and the Count of Poppi, and his own wish to redeem the barrenness of his campaign by a successful stroke, made him desire to fight at least one pitched battle before his return. His long delays had, however, enabled Florence to collect a considerable army, reinforced by the Papal troops. It was now posted on the Florentine borders at Anghiari, where it stood on the defensive, and would have permitted

Piccinino to retire to Lombardy unhindered if he had wished. But Piccinino heard that the Florentine generals were divided amongst themselves, refusing to obey the Commissioners, Neri Capponi and Bernardetto de' Medici, and that their camp was in much disorder. He attempted, therefore, to make a surprise attack on the afternoon of June 29th. Fortunately his coming was perceived; the Florentine army had time to fall into hasty position, behind the shelter of a stream on the slope of the hill on which Anghiari stands; and after a short contest Piccinino had to withdraw in disorder, leaving an immense number of prisoners behind. Had the victory been followed up, Piccinino himself might have been captured; but the Florentine soldiers were more intent on securing their own prisoners than on pressing forward. Two days later, however, Borgo S. Sepolcro, which had been garrisoned by Piccinino, surrendered, and was restored to its proper owner, the Pope; the Florentine places which Piccinino had captured were then recovered, and punishment was meted out to the Count of Poppi.

Florence was now quite willing for a peace, and welcomed that which Sforza negotiated at Cavriana in 1441, after another successful campaign in Lombardy. Florence had spent much money on the war, and was glad of a respite to enable her to re-establish her finances. On the whole, its results had been satisfactory to her, and particularly to the Medicean party. Opportunities for rejoicing over a military victory had of late been rare; this one was made the most of, and it gave much prestige to the Government, while a decided territorial gain had been made at the expense of the

Count of Poppi. From this time too the exiles were no longer dangerous; the attitude of Florence while they were at her gates greatly increased the sense of security enjoyed by the ruling party. The victory of Anghiari and the subsequent peace established Cosimo's power in Florence, which before this time had more than once trembled in the balance.

Another advantage gained by Cosimo was the confirmation of the alliance with Sforza, which from this time became a permanent part of Florentine policy. The battle of Anghiari had been won mainly by Sforzescan troops; Florence had been taught how helpless she was without Sforza's services; Sforza had learned how faithful and, on the whole, self-sacrificing Florence could be towards an ally whom she appreciated. Sforza's importance had been greatly increased by the negotiations at Cavriana, where he acted as arbiter, and where "all the Italian states seemed to be in his hands." He was now the husband of Bianca Visconti, the lord of Cremona and Pontremoli, which he received from Visconti as his daughter's dowry, and the probable successor to Milan. He was no longer, therefore, a mere soldier, to be employed or dismissed at pleasure, but a considerable power amongst the Italian states, whose alliance was well worth the trouble that Florence had taken to preserve it.

Although Lucca had escaped, the Medicean Government had been able to make some substantial additions to the Florentine territory. Monte Carlo and Uzzano, which had been won from Lucca, were important posts on the Lucchese bank of the River Nievole, and formed a *pied-à-terre*, which might prove useful in a future war.

Motrone, the other fortress obtained from Lucca, gave Florence a new coast station. In 1436, Florence recovered Rocca S. Casciano, on the Romagnol borders, which had been appropriated by the lords of Forlì. On this subject Cosimo was involved in a dispute with the Pope, who claimed it himself, and Lorenzo de' Medici had to be despatched on a special mission to him to arrange the affair.

Much more important was the reduction of the property of the Count of Poppi in the Casentino to complete dependence on the Republic. From henceforth Florence held the whole upper valley of the Arno, and was far better secured from attack on the Romagnol borders. Another family, the Pietramala of Montedoglio, in the upper valley of the Tiber, who were also ricommandati to Florence, and rebels in 1441, had their property taken from them and placed directly under the Republic. In the same district the possession of Borgo S. Sepolcro had been for some time in dispute between the Pope and the Count of Poppi. Shortly after the fall of the Count, it was purchased by Florence from the Pope for 25,000 florins. To save the Papal dignity it was said to be only pledged; but it was unlikely that any future Pope would want to redeem it. Cosimo, who thought that so considerable a town, placed in a commanding position in the Tiber valley, was worth some sacrifice, negotiated the sale, and further increased the obligations of the Republic towards himself by advancing the purchase money.

With his position established at home, and secure from the attacks of the exiles without, Cosimo was able to draw the reins of foreign policy more closely into his own hands, and, going beyond the mere opportunism with which he had so far contented himself, to embark with deliberate purpose upon a constructive policy, adapted to meet the necessities of the time in the way which he thought best, and largely shaped by his own ideas and individuality. The object of this constructive policy was to establish such a balance between the Italian powers, to "reduce them to such an equality," that no one single state should be able to outweigh a league of the others. This would secure the existence, the safety, and even the independence of Florence, and in so doing secure the position of himself and his family at the head of the Republic.

The germ of the idea of a "Balance of Power" had long existed in Italy, though nowhere else in Europe. There was a kind of federal idea amongst the Italian states, the sense of a Commonwealth existing among them, which led them to form into leagues to suppress any one member of the Commonwealth that showed itself powerful enough to threaten the existence of the others. So for half a century the Republics of Venice and Florence had combined against Visconti. This was indeed the first appearance of that theory of the "Balance of Power" which dominated the politics of Europe from the beginning of the sixteenth century until the French Revolution. It was Cosimo who gave form and substance to the floating idea, converting a merely general notion into an elaborately detailed system; negotiating, intriguing, combining, and shifting alliances, with the view, not only to prevent one power from absorbing the others, but so to equalise the powers that even the combination of two should not seriously threaten the equilibrium of the Balance. When in fact a dangerous combination of two powers actually took place, Cosimo's resource was to call in aid from without,—to call in France to weigh down the Balance against Venice and Naples. But this was an extreme measure, and for many years Cosimo contrived to maintain the Balance by the formation of an inter-Italian league against the state or states which were at the moment dangerously powerful.

Now that Visconti was growing old, it was Alfonso of Naples who, having finally driven the Angevins out of his kingdom, had become the threatening factor in Italian politics. His restless ambition was a serious danger to peace; for, as Visconti said, "the state of Naples is not like others, but must be held sword in hand; so that Alfonso cannot rest quiet, but must either lose all or conquer all." More especially did he seem dangerous to Florence, the old adherent of the Angevin cause, and to Sforza, who was not only a friend of the Angevins, having held estates under them in Naples, whose possession he would not let go without a struggle, but was also continually threatening the Neapolitan borders from his position in the March. Their common enmity to Alfonso drew Sforza and Florence closer together; Cosimo was determined to keep Sforza in the March as a check upon Alfonso, and in the future, after Visconti should be dead, to establish him at Milan as a barrier between Florence and Venice, in whom Cosimo was already beginning to recognise a rival and future enemy. For the present, however, he intended to keep up the Venetian alliance, even at some sacrifice to Florence, in order to secure Venetian support and, still more, Venetian wealth for Sforza.

Venice was, in fact, the only ally for Florence and Sforza upon whom Cosimo could count. The Pope, to whom Sforza's possession of the March was even more intolerable than it was to Alfonso, had only suffered it as long as Visconti was threatening the Papal States, and had been looking out for an opportunity to put an end to it. Visconti still maintained his alliance with Alfonso, and had used the influence which, at the moment of their reconciliation, he possessed over Sforza to prevent him from succouring the Angevins in their last struggles. Besides, Visconti was now even more jealous of Sforza than he had been before he was actually Bianca's husband, and was full of suspicion that his son-in-law would try to seize Bianca's inheritance before it fell to him in the course of nature. It was therefore Visconti who, by lending him the services of Piccinino, afforded the Pope the opportunity he sought for an attack on the March. Cosimo used every endeavour to reconcile Sforza and the Pope; in 1441 he contrived to patch up a peace which Eugenius at once evaded; in 1442 he sent his cousin, Bernadetto de' Medici, a capable diplomat, into the March, to negotiate between Piccinino and Sforza. Bernadetto twice succeeded in making truces, which Piccinino received Papal dispensation to break as soon as they were made.

All this time the Pope was still residing in Florence; but as he became less friendly towards his hosts, he grew anxious to return to Rome, which he could not do so long as Sforza was all-powerful in the Papal States, and Naples was in the hands of his old enemy, Alfonso. But the Pope would not hesitate to abandon the Angevin cause, to which he was pledged, and to seek a *rapproche-*

ment with Alfonso, if by this means he might obtain his desires. René of Anjou, after leaving Naples, returned to Provence, and on his way visited Florence, where he received plenty of condolence, but no practical assistance. Eugenius indeed bestowed the investiture of Naples upon him, but this was a mere formality, intended to throw dust into the eyes of René's friends in France. René felt that his cause was hopeless, and retired into Provence. The final blow to all hopes of a reconciliation was struck when, early in 1443, the Pope announced his intention of quitting Florence and returning to Rome.

The event which had ultimately led Eugenius to this decision was the sudden, and, to the general public, unexplained execution of a Condottiere captain, Baldaccio d'Anghiari. Baldaccio, who had been in the service of Florence during the recent war, was visiting the city, and was summoned by the Signory to the Palace, ostensibly on military business. While talking to the Gonfalonier, he was set upon and seized by a band of armed men, who flung him from the window into the courtyard beneath, where the executioner immediately decapitated him. An act of such unusual violence caused a great sensation in Florence, where judicial murders were as a rule accomplished with a decent privacy. The reason stated by the Signory was Baldaccio's disobedience to their commands while in their service, but the public were not slow in attributing to it a deeper political importance. It was believed that Cosimo was afraid of the friendship between the Condottiere and Neri Capponi, and had therefore put an end to it in this summary fashion. The real reason, however, escaped the people, who did not know that Baldaccio had but the day before his death been taken into pay by the Pope, who had at once given him 80,000 florins. Cosimo of course understood that Baldaccio was to be used to fight against Sforza, and was therefore determined to get rid of him by fair means or foul. The Pope was obliged to conceal his anger while he was still at Cosimo's mercy; but he determined to set himself free by leaving Florence as soon as possible.

The announcement of his decision was equivalent to a statement that he meant to put himself under the protection of Alfonso, and that his enmity to Sforza was irremediable. "The portent of our future misfortunes!" exclaimed the Florentines, and they all urged the Pope to reconsider his decision. The Venetian ambassadors then in Florence went so far as to suggest that Eugenius should be detained by force, and some Florentines were of their opinion; but Cosimo felt that this would only be a useless insult, and finally the Pope was allowed to depart, outwardly still on good terms with the Republic.

But the League between Eugenius and Alfonso which Florence dreaded was published immediately afterwards; the investiture of Alfonso with Naples being the price paid by Eugenius for his safe return to Rome and for aid against Sforza. Alfonso invaded the March in person, where Piccinino and the Papal troops aided him. Sforza, totally unable to hold his own against so many enemies, seemed to be about to lose all his dominions.

To save him a new ally was needed. Bologna, which under the Bentivogli had just recovered her independence, and was at war with Visconti, was taken into the League; but this measure, though popular in

Florence, where the independence of Bologna was always looked on favourably, was rather a source of weakness than of strength to Sforza, since it diverted the troops of the League from his aid to that of Bologna.

A new ally for Sforza was, however, shortly discovered in Visconti himself, who was already willing to change sides. He did not wish to crush Sforza completely, nor to let Piccinino have too much success; still more was he afraid of Alfonso's League with the Pope. First he tried to persuade Alfonso to leave the March; then he openly joined the League of the two Republics and Sforza, a step which effectually frightened Alfonso home to Naples. The independence of Bologna having by this time been secured, the troops of the League were able to join Sforza in the March. With their aid he inflicted a crushing defeat on Piccinino and the Papal troops, now left without Alfonso's support. Encouraged by Sforza's success, Venice and Florence were persuaded to give him further supplies of money. Visconti was still more active in his cause. He went so far as to suggest to the Republics that Alfonso should be expelled from Naples, when Sforza had been secured in the March; he even negotiated with René of Anjou for the same purpose. Finally, by a clever feint, he withdrew Piccinino from the March, and during his absence Sforza attacked and destroyed the old general's army. Piccinino died heart-broken at the triumph of his rival and the treachery of his master. Eugenius, left defenceless and terrified, was willing to listen to Cosimo's exhortations to peace. Negotiations were opened at Perugia, in which Cosimo, though not present, was practically the guiding spirit. A treaty was drawn up by which Sforza was to keep a great part of the March; details were to be settled by the arbitration of a Commission of Cardinals, with Cosimo and Neri Capponi. Once more Cosimo seemed to have saved Sforza and to have secured peace for Italy. This had been his first trial of the system of the Balance of Power. The alliance of the Pope and Alfonso had been outweighed by detaching Visconti from it, and obtaining his aid for Sforza. So far the system was acting well.

And, as long as Visconti maintained his favourable attitude, the Pope and Alfonso were awed into keeping the peace. For a time Visconti seemed quite alienated from Alfonso; he went so far as to offer aid to the Dauphin in case the latter would invade Italy in favour of the Angevin claimant to Naples. We find him offering to allow Cosimo to act as he pleased towards Piombino, Lucca and Siena, if Cosimo would reciprocally grant him a free hand for some design of his, presumably that of a French invasion. But this state of things could not last long. There could be no real repose so long as Eugenius and Alfonso were ready to strain every nerve to drive Sforza from the March, and Visconti's jealousy of his son-in-law only slept to be re-awakened. Without Piccinino, Visconti felt himself at Sforza's mercy; the closeness of the bond which held Sforza to the League, and which no blandishments of his could weaken, terrified him. Sforza wished to keep his hold both on Visconti and on the League at once; but Visconti could not peaceably share a servant with the Republics, nor, as he said, would he consent to be "a slave to Count Francesco" (Sforza). He began to form a new army under the sons of Piccinino; early in 1445 Venice was already warning Sforza that Visconti had secret designs on Cremona, Bianca's dowry town, and in the summer he stirred up a revolt in Bologna, "in the name of the Church," against Cosimo's friends, the Bentivogli. With the aid of the troops of the League, the Bentivogli were able to maintain the independence of Bologna, but this affair was the sign that Visconti had again come to an understanding with the Pope against Sforza. In spite of Cosimo's schemes and struggles to prevent it, the very alliance that he dreaded, that of Alfonso, Visconti and the Pope, was formed, the Pope breaking finally with the Angevin cause by promising the reversion of Naples to Alfonso's illegitimate son, Ferrante.

The purpose of this new alliance appeared to be a war of extermination against Sforza. Visconti, with a fine assumption of disinterestedness, threw the blame on Sforza's ambition; if Sforza were allowed to retain the March, he declared, he would only "want more, for his nature, is not like that of a king, to remain content with what he possesses; since those who are not rulers by nature the more they have the more they want, and there is never any end to their desires. . . . Sforza will want Calabria as well as the March." And, Visconti added, with what sounds like irony from the meanest and greediest of the "natural" rulers,—"it seems better to me to pay obedience to a natural king" (such as Alfonso), "than to be in peril of coming under a community in which there are shoemakers and tailors, and all sorts and conditions of men" (such as Florence), "or under adventurers who do not know who their own fathers were" (such as Sforza).

The condition of Sforza's affairs was almost hopeless; it seemed impossible to detach any of his enemies from the League against him. Eugenius was irreconcilable; the action of Cosimo in supporting the independence of Bologna, and restoring the Bentivogli, when their line seemed to be threatened with extinction, had still further alienated him. An open quarrel almost broke out between the Pope and the Republic, when the former seized and imprisoned Bernadetto de' Medici, Florentine ambassador to Naples, on his way through Rome, in defiance of his safe-conduct. Diplomacy failed to release him, and reprisals had to be resorted to before he was set free. Visconti meanwhile attacked Cremona, declaring that Sforza had promised to restore it in return for a money dowry, and was now refusing to keep his promise. He continued his attacks on Bologna, and hoping to draw off Florence from its defence, sent troops to threaten Pontremoli, the second of Sforza's dowry towns. In the March, Sforza was rapidly losing all he possessed to the Neapolitan and Papal armies. Twice, in the winter of 1445-46, he visited Florence to beg for money; Cosimo gave him all that he could get, but it was not nearly enough to satisfy him.

Cosimo's only resource was to fall back upon Venice, which, though his ally and Sforza's, had so far shown herself very indifferent to Sforza's fortunes. Cosimo distrusted Venice, but he was obliged to make use of her in his necessity. Twice Neri Capponi was sent on special missions to Venice to urge her to more active measures, but in vain; finally, Cosimo hit upon the expedient of inducing Venice to send to Visconti a joint embassy with Florence; Visconti fell into the trap, received the ambassadors with great rudeness, and thus roused the anger of Venice against himself. She entered vigorously into the war; and her Condottiere, Michele Sforza, administered a crushing defeat to the Milanese at Casalmaggiore in September (1446). This victory secured Cremona, forced Visconti to recall his troops from the attack of Pontremoli, and enormously strengthened Sforza's position in the March. Venice, having tasted success, desired more; her army passed Crema, crossed the Adda, and advanced to within a few miles of Milan, threatening Visconti's capital itself. Again Cosimo's Balance of Power had proved successful; with the aid of Venice, Florence and Sforza could counterbalance Visconti, Alfonso, and the Pope.

But the victory of Casalmaggiore was the signal for the beginning of a complete revolution in Italian politics. Its immediate effect was to produce distrust and suspicion between Sforza and Venice. Venice had won a great battle without Sforza's aid; she was therefore inclined to depreciate his military value, and indeed his failures in the March gave her an excuse. So easily was she defeating Visconti, that she was also led to underrate his powers of resistance, and to think that she might turn him out of Milan; and then, why give Milan over to Sforza? why not appropriate the prey herself? Sforza perfectly understood her feelings; he knew that if she continued to be successful, Milan would lie entirely at her disposal. Venice was already beginning to withhold the pecuniary support she had promised him; Cremona was practically at her mercy, should she at any moment declare herself his enemy.

As was natural, he looked to Visconti for help in this danger.

Visconti, rendered desperate by his reverses, was ready to seek help anywhere. He made large offers to Venice; he turned again to France, begged for a French expedition against Venice, for French mediation to detach Florence from the Venetian alliance; he would let the Dauphin have Asti and Genoa; he would even, he hinted, give up the cause of his ally Alfonso, and permit a restoration of the Angevins to Naples. But above all he turned to Cosimo, seeking his good offices for a reconciliation with Sforza.

This was the turning-point in the history of Cosimo's foreign policy. So far he had remained true to the old alliance of Florence with Venice. Now the breach between Venice and Sforza led to his deserting the Venetian alliance, and ranging himself and Florence on the side of Sforza, even of Visconti, against Venice. The whole process of the change occupied some years, but it took Cosimo and Sforza only a few months to determine upon it.

A gradual separation of interests between Venice and Florence, and particularly between Venice and Cosimo, might long have been observed by a careful eye. From the time that they disagreed over Sforza's services; from the time in fact of Cosimo's unsuccessful mission to Venice in 1438, there had been a growing division. The breach was temporarily covered over, but it was not healed. Cosimo well understood that the interests of two rival commercial states could not be made permanently to coincide; he had also been taught, by some years' experience of the grasping, avaricious character of

Venice, that the ambition of the Sea-Republic was more to be dreaded than any other danger which might threaten the equilibrium of the Italian states. Tyrants, greedy and cunning like Visconti, monarchs, restless and ambitious like Alfonso, might arise; but they would die and their power come to an end; Venice, as a corporation, never died, and she conquered always to retain. Florence had said in a moment of anger that Venice wanted to acquire the dominion over all Italy; Cosimo knew the charge to be substantially true, and understood that the only really safe policy for Florence was to head a league which should devote itself to keeping down the rising ambition of Venice, now a greater danger to the Balance of Power than were Alfonso and Visconti. Cosimo preferred to be on the same side as Visconti, even as Alfonso, if only Venice might thus be held in check.

At Visconti's request, therefore, he undertook the task of mediation between him and Sforza. Throughout the winter of 1446-47 numerous letters passed between them, in which Cosimo urged Sforza to break off his hollow alliance with Venice, and be reconciled to his father-in-law. Sforza should, Cosimo said, "suit himself to the times, and do what he found necessary." By November a secret understanding had been reached; Sforza made a truce with the Papal army, and allowed some troops going to the relief of Milan to pass through the March. Early next year, Visconti was ordering his soldiers not to attack Cremona, while the ill-feeling between Sforza and Venice was increasing. They quarrelled about the disposition of their Condottieri; then Sforza reproached Venice for failing to supply him with money, and protested against the large number of Venetian troops stationed in the Cremonese district, whose presence he looked upon as a threat. Venice too became suspicious of Sforza, in spite of his continual protests of fidelity. She continued her campaign near Milan, kept her hold over the Cremonese district, and prepared for the worst. Early in 1447, a discontented servant of Sforza's revealed to her the full extent of his treachery. She retorted at once by a surprise attack upon Cremona, which was very nearly successful. Sforza protested, but the breach between them was final; and Sforza at last yielded to Visconti's exhortations, entered into an alliance with him and Alfonso, and promised to march into Lombardy to his assistance.

The open breach between Venice and Sforza made it necessary for Florence to decide whose side she would take, and, as Cosimo had very clearly foreseen, it was towards Venice that the Florentines inclined. For years they had been pouring out money to Sforza to defend them against Visconti; now that Visconti seemed powerless they were growing unwilling to subsidise the Condottiere any longer. They could not see that Sforza's alliance did them much good; they felt as if their money were wasted on him. His greediness and selfishness made him unpopular. "The people said," wrote the chronicler Cavalcanti, Sforza's bitter opponent, "we are made to submit to an unworthy tyranny. Our fathers liberated us from servitude to the Duke of Athens; but now we are made subject to the off-shoot of that mean Castle of Cottignola" (the cradle of Sforza's family). "This tyrant does not make requests of us, but commands us outright. We have become slaves to Count Francesco!"

On the other hand, the attitude of Venice towards the city of Milan, offering to help her establish a Milanese Republic on the fall of Visconti, was pleasing to the Republican sentiments of the Florentines. Sforza's confidential agent in Florence, Nicodemo, had, as early as November 1446, warned him that the Florentines suspected him, and only Cosimo favoured him. They were refusing to give him money; Cosimo, who, as an official for the administration of the Monte Comune, was able to obtain supplies, had great difficulty in procuring his own re-election to that office, although Sforza's agent and friends in Florence did all they could for him. Cosimo himself told Nicodemo that he could not "force this people," that what he was already doing for Sforza was enough to endanger his own head if it were discovered. Florence perhaps thought that she could keep Sforza faithful to her, without paying for his fidelity; even Cosimo, Nicodemo wrote, fancied that whatever he did he would always be able "to keep you" (Sforza) "in his service." Quite early in 1447, when their trust in Sforza began to fail, the Signory had warned Venice to keep a sharp look-out on him, since rumours of his treachery were getting abroad. Florence was yet more agitated by the discovery of Visconti's intrigues with France. The Dauphin was said to be contemplating an invasion of Italy in Visconti's favour. He had promised not to interfere with Florence herself, the ancient ally of France; but his coming must necessarily revolutionise Italian affairs.

When the final breach occurred, a sharp opposition between two rival parties in Florence became apparent. Cosimo headed the one, Neri Capponi was the leader of the other. The letters of Nicodemo show how keenly the battle was contested. Sforza demanded money; the proposals of Cosimo to grant him subsidies failed to pass the Florentine Councils. Cosimo had to resort to somewhat shady financial-political transactions in order to obtain anything for him. In vain he urged upon the Florentines the advantages of a break with Venice and an alliance with Sforza, pointing out that when Sforza should have succeeded to Milan he would no longer need Florentine money, nor disturb the quiet of Tuscany from the neighbouring March; that to enable Venice to appropriate Milan was the most suicidal policy possible; that Florence was no longer bound by her engagements to Venice, which were purely defensive, since Venice had begun to act upon the offensive against Visconti.

A further difficulty for Cosimo was the fear which Florence was beginning to entertain of the threatening attitude of Alfonso, who, though he was now in negotiation with Sforza for an accommodation of the affairs of the March, was showing himself uncompromisingly hostile to the two Republics, refused proposed negotiations, and threatened an invasion of Tuscany, in order, he said, to force Florence to abandon the Venetian alliance. Florence hesitated; in spite of the pressure put upon her by Venice, which "day and night" urged her to make military preparations, she took no active steps. Sforza, who understood how the direction of her policy hung in the balance, urged Alfonso to show himself more conciliatory, lest he should force her to throw herself into the arms of Venice in order to defend herself against him. Sforza hoped rather by conciliatory measures to detach her from Venice; "Cosimo and others," he wrote to Alfonso, "have sent to tell me that in this manner it may be possible to induce dissension between Florence and Venice."

Yet another difficulty for Cosimo lay in the attitude of the new Pope, Nicolas V., towards Sforza. Florence had rejoiced at the death of Eugenius as at "good news," for of late years he had become uncompromisingly hostile to her. She rejoiced still more at the appointment of his successor, Tommaso Parentucelli, who had spent some years of his youth in Florence, when he was tutor to the sons of Palla Strozzi, and who was closely bound to the Republic, and especially to Cosimo, by ties of personal friendship. "The Pope cordially loves Cosimo," wrote a contemporary; "I am certain that he will place everything in his disposition, for there is no one in the world in whom he trusts so much as he does in Cosimo." Yet, though he allowed Cosimo to reconcile him with Bologna, and, expressing himself anxious for a general peace, opened public negotiations at Ferrara, he, like Eugenius, was obstinate on the question of the March. Sforza had already promised to surrender a great part of that disputed province to Eugenius, in return for a subsidy to be paid by the Pope and Alfonso, which would enable him to go to Lombardy for the relief of Visconti; but Nicolas V. demanded harder terms, and an endless haggling went on, Alfonso wavering between the two parties. Sforza held out all the spring, refusing to go to Lombardy without the subsidy, and refusing to surrender the March towns which Nicolas wanted. The position was becoming strained; Visconti, beginning to suspect Sforza of playing him false, and of meaning to come to Milan "as a lord, not as a hired soldier," held back money from him, and kept up his coquetting with France. Venice meanwhile pushed her conquests further and further; already, as Cosimo pointed out to Sforza, he would not be able to secure a share in "the Lombard cake," without giving Venice a good slice out of it. Cosimo left no persuasions untried to hasten Sforza's steps towards Lombardy; he said to Nicodemo, "I wish that the Count would attend to one business only, and that is his expedition into Lombardy, and leave everything else alone. . . . I wish the Count would show to the Duke" (Visconti) "that he thinks of nothing but his safety, and would give up Zesi, which is really of no value to him, to the Pope." Cosimo felt how much more important Milan was than the small towns in the March for which Sforza was delaying; and he knew that a little longer delay would involve the loss of Milan. Venice was pressing it hard, and Visconti's health showed signs of giving way. Sforza must be in Milan when Visconti died, Cosimo urged; as Sforza himself had said not long before, "he is indeed to be pitied who cannot be present at the wedding of his own wife."

At last Sforza was persuaded to accept what terms he could get from the Pope, and set out on his march northwards. On the way news reached him of his father-in-law's fatal illness; a little later he received tidings that Visconti was dead. He died as he had lived, intriguing with all parties at once, and faithful to none; but his death ended a definite phase in Italian politics, —the period of the League of the two Republics in defence of their liberty, which had been so long threatened by him and his father. From henceforth there was no pressure from without to keep the Republics together, and they drifted into opposition, as their commercial and political rivalry naturally led them to do. The alliance with Venice occupied the first part of Cosimo's rule in Florence; his later years were largely taken up with the quarrels of the two Republics.

CHAPTER IV

FOREIGN POLICY FROM 1447 TO 1464—THE CONQUEST OF MILAN FOR SFORZA—THE FRENCH AND MILANESE ALLIANCES

THE death of Visconti left the Florentines with a new political problem to solve,—what part they were to take in settling who should be the future ruler of Milan. There were various claimants whose designs Florence, as an Italian state, could not favour: the Duke of Orleans (through a female ancestor), the Emperor, who claimed as suzerain, and Alfonso of Naples, to whom Visconti, in spite of his recent reconciliation with Sforza, had attempted to leave his Duchy by will. And, in spite of her old alliance with Venice, Florence could not consent that the rival Republic should enormously increase her dominions by adding to them Milan and all western Lombardy. Two solutions remained; one was advocated by the old, oligarchical, conservative party in Florence, led by Neri Capponi and Giannozzo Manetti, the other by the new, enterprising, almost radical party, led by the Medici. The former desired that Milan, as she herself wished, should be made into a Republic; that the league with Venice should be maintained, and that Venice should be bribed off from wanting Milan for herself by a large share in the "Lombard cake." The latter, who foresaw that Venice must have all or none, were for breaking definitely with her, and giving Milan and its Duchy wholly to Francesco Sforza. The conservative party, remembering the Visconti, dreaded a despotism, which they thought must of its nature be always opposed to a Republic, and dreaded, above all, a military despotism in the hands of a soldier like Sforza. The Radical party, themselves opposed to oligarchies, and therefore with little sympathy for Venice as a fellow-Republic, hoped in Sforza to set up a barrier between Florence and Venice, and one far more powerful than an infant Milanese Republic, just struggling into life, could interpose. Unfortunately for Cosimo, the lower classes, usually on his side, were in this crisis on the side of the opposition. To them the alliance with Sforza appeared to mean constant taxation, and, so far as they could see, very little came of all their sacrifices. By the Venetian League Florence had at least obtained a certain respect and reputation; by her championship of Sforza since 1441 Florence had got nothing but expense and disappointments. The people declared that "this tyrant Visconti has kept all Italy in arms for twenty-four years; but God grant that there may not arise a greater one, as already we see Count Francesco wishes to be!"

The whole question was complicated and rendered far more difficult by the action of Alfonso. For some months he had been designing an attack on Florence, for which, as the constant friend of the Angevins, he cherished a bitter hatred, with the ostensible object of forcing her to detach herself from her alliance with Venice. Before Visconti's death, some soldiers in Alfonso's pay had made a sudden attack upon Cennina, a Florentine fortress in the upper Val d'Arno, had captured it, and were only expelled with difficulty. Just after Visconti's death, Alfonso, having procured from the Sienese permission for the passage of his troops, crossed their territory into the district of Volterra, and captured several castles in that neighbourhood. A Dieci of War was hastily elected in Florence, the frontier forts garrisoned, and Federigo of Urbino was taken into the Florentine service; but Alfonso's attack had been so unexpected that for a time little could be done to check him. As usual, Florence knew her weakest point to be the Pisan district, and towards this Alfonso soon moved. Here again he took several castles, but, as winter advanced, was obliged to encamp near the coast, where he could receive supplies from Naples by sea, and remained inactive until the spring.

Although Alfonso had intended by this invasion to detach Florence from the Venetian alliance, the effect of it was exactly opposite. As Sforza had foreseen and warned Alfonso, Florence was on the contrary driven into the arms of Venice, just at the moment when she was wavering. Cosimo was powerless to withstand the popular determination to cling to the League, and to get what help could be got from Venice, leaving the Milanese question to settle itself. Venice replied to the requests of Florence for help by vague promises, and a declaration of war against Alfonso; but her whole energies were really bent upon Lombardy, where she was engaged in a hand-to-hand struggle with Sforza, then acting as general to the "Milanese Republic," and she was glad to buy off possible interference from Florence so cheaply.

The only possible line of policy left to Cosimo was to keep up by every means in his power the enmity between Alfonso and Venice; for, were these two to agree in uniting against Sforza, and dividing Milan between them, his cause must certainly be lost. With this purpose in view, Cosimo suggested to Venice that René of Anjou should be invited into Italy to attack Naples, and call Alfonso off from Tuscany. Venice listened, made half-promises, and did nothing; she had in fact nothing to gain by keeping up Alfonso's enmity to herself. Cosimo even sent one of the Pazzi family, with whom René was very friendly, to the Angevin Court, to make offers to the king on behalf of the two Republics. There was little sincerity, however, in the affair, which was probably rather a threat to Alfonso, and a means of keeping him at enmity with Venice, than a serious negotiation. Cosimo knew well enough, as Sforza pointed out, that to bring René into Italy was only to show the way there to another claimant to the Duchy of Milan, the Duke of Orleans, who was quite ready to enforce his claim, and whom Venice sometimes threatened to recognise as Duke in opposition to Sforza.

On the other hand, the opposition party in Florence were endeavouring, all through the early part of the year 1448, to negotiate a general peace between Venice, Florence, and Alfonso, leaving out Sforza. For this purpose they were constantly trying to get embassies sent to Alfonso and Venice, and Cosimo was as constantly trying to frustrate these efforts. On one occasion, Cosimo substituted Neri Capponi as envoy to Venice for two ambassadors, who were set on peace with Venice and Alfonso only, while Neri wished for an accommodation between Venice and Sforza. At the same time, Florence made direct offers of peace to Alfonso, which the Venetian ambassadors contrived to make him reject, since Venice was not included in them. Cosimo's aim was, in fact, to arrange a peace between Sforza and Venice, before Venice had time to draw towards Alfonso, and this he was successful in effecting. From April until October, secret negotiations were conducted through him at Florence; in September a signal victory by Sforza over the Venetian troops made the Republic willing to give way, and allow herself to be bribed with the offer of several Lombard towns, leaving Milan to Sforza. Venice and Sforza united their troops to force Milan into submission; and Cosimo, now that he thought Sforza was in a fair way to acquire Milan, even allowed some Florentine troops to be sent into the service of Venice. Sforza was able to press Milan hard, almost blockading the city, and Cosimo could allow the sham negotiations with René to drop.

Meanwhile, Cosimo's hands had been set free by the complete failure of the Neapolitan invasion. Alfonso had taken Castiglione della Pescaja, an important coast-town, which had long been ricommandato to Florence; but he had not succeeded in inducing Rinaldo Orsini, the ruler of Piombino, to enter into a league with him against Florence. He had therefore laid siege to Piombino, hoping to take and keep it permanently as a basis for future action in Tuscany. Orsini appealed to

Florence for help, and Florence rose to the occasion. Her army was increased and strengthened, and, with Neri Capponi as Commissioner, marched to hinder Alfonso's operations. Meanwhile, Alfonso's army was worn out by the long campaign, and the bad climate of the Piombese coast marshes. He made a final assault upon the town in September (1448), but it was a failure, and he was obliged to retire from Tuscany, leaving a large number of his troops dead behind him.

Cosimo's task seemed easy and straightforward now. Neri Capponi, finding Venice and Sforza in alliance, was obliged to drop the idea of a Milanese Republic, and to a certain extent withdraw his opposition. In April (1449) we hear from Sforza's permanent agent in Florence, Nicodemo, that two or three powerful opponents had been won over to his side. Still Cosimo could not contrive to rouse any enthusiasm in Florence in Sforza's favour. In June, Nicodemo assured his master that no one but Cosimo really cared for his interests; "and the more Cosimo urges, the more the others hold back; and one spiteful person is more able to spoil an undertaking than ten favourable to carry it through." The fact was that Sforza was still pressing the Republic for money. Cosimo granted him vast sums out of his private purse, and lent him the money of the Commune, over which, as an official of the Monte, he had control; but Sforza was insatiable. Again and again he promised to ask for no more; and again and again he broke his promise and made fresh demands. Still less likely was he to find favour in Florence, when, towards the end of the year, a fresh quarrel broke out between him and his new ally, Venice. For Sforza, as he came nearer to the conquest of Milan, distrusted Venice more and more. Venice, although during this year she had been carrying on a naval war against Alfonso's Sicilian towns, was continually in negotiation with him and with the Milanese republicans. At length, in October, a treaty between Milan and Venice was announced, which was to secure the independence of Milan, while Sforza was to be bribed with an offer of some of the west Lombard towns. Venice, however, had shown her hand too plainly; it was obvious that she meant to secure Milan herself, so soon as Sforza had laid down arms. Sforza, seeing through the pretence, delayed his acceptance of the treaty, meanwhile making fresh appeals to Cosimo for money, and for negotiations in his favour. Finally he refused to ratify the treaty; and, in spite of the attempts of Venice to hinder him, pressed the siege of Milan more closely.

Venice pretended to conciliate Florence by the offer of a place in her new league with the Milanese Republic, and Cosimo could not prevent the despatch of an embassy from Florence to Venice on the subject. All he could do was to delay negotiations as long as possible, hoping that Sforza might obtain some signal success which should distract the Florentines from their leanings to Venice. He was not disappointed; in February 1450 Milan gave itself up to Sforza, and accepted him as her Duke. Exactly as Cosimo expected, the effect of Sforza's success acted like magic on the Florentines; they forgot their fear of Venice, expressed themselves delighted at Sforza's conquest, and were ready to despatch an influential embassy, including Neri Capponi and Piero de' Medici, Cosimo's eldest son, to recognise him as Duke, and congratulate him without delay.

Cosimo had good reason to rejoice; the end towards which he had been working during the past ten years was reached at last; Francesco Sforza was lord of Milan, and had obtained that position so largely by means of Cosimo's support and aid that his interests were inextricably bound up with those of the Medici house. At the same time, Sforza's success meant the success of Cosimo's home as well as foreign policy; it strengthened enormously the Medicean party in Florence. This the Venetians knew very well when they said that, in order to separate Florence from Sforza, it was necessary to work directly through the Florentine Signory, in which members of the opposition might be found; for it was useless to attempt to detach Cosimo himself from Sforza, since it was through Sforza that he had actually obtained his own position in Florence. Venice, acting on this principle, tried to draw Florence from her Milanese leanings through Neri Capponi, who, together with Piero de' Medici, was sent on from Milan to Venice, ostensibly to open negotiations there in favour of Sforza. Cosimo, fearing what Neri might do, and unable to persuade the Signory, who still hankered after the Venetian alliance, to recall the ambassadors, sent private commands to his son to leave Venice; and Neri, afraid of the responsibility of treating alone, followed Piero home. This was in fact a sign of the final breach between the two Republics, which had long been widening, but was now completely opened, not to be healed again for many years. Venice was furious at this mark of want of respect shown her by Florence, which a short time since had been practically dependent on her; she realised that it was through Florence that she had lost Milan, and she conceived the bitterest hatred against her old friend Cosimo, who had outreached her in her own arts.

Cosimo, in fact, knew that Venice and Alfonso were drawing nearer to each other, out of their common enmity to Sforza and himself. Negotiations had been proceeding between them for some time, and they culminated in an alliance, published in July 1450, an alliance which divided Italy at last into two distinct camps,—Florence and Milan against Venice and Naples. Only a few days previous to it a treaty of peace had been signed between Florence and Alfonso, but this was obviously little more than a truce to enable both parties to recover from their late struggle; and Florence needed the repose so greatly that she submitted, rather than not obtain the treaty, to leave Castiglione della Pescaja in Alfonso's hands for the present.

The first portent of the coming hostilities appeared in 1451, when a joint Embassy from Naples and Venice visited Florence, offering Florence a place in their League if she would give up the cause of Sforza, and complaining bitterly of the help which Florence had afforded him in his conquest of Milan, in violation of her League with Venice. Cosimo, for once emerging from the political obscurity in which he shrouded himself, answered the complaints in person at a public audience, protesting that Florence had not broken with Venice, but that it was Venice which, in 1449, had broken with their common ally, Sforza. There was plenty of sophistical self-justification on both sides; but the ultimate result was that Florence refused the offer, and decided to adhere to Sforza; a League for mutual defence was shortly afterwards concluded (August 1451). Venice and Alfonso retaliated by exiling all Florentine residents from their respective dominions, a blow aimed at the commerce of Florence, and severely felt by her, as was shown by an immediate fall in the value of the Monte Comune. Venice tried to procure other allies in Italy; she intrigued in Milan and others of Sforza's towns in the hope of raising revolts; she attempted, but in vain, to undermine the authority of Cosimo's allies, the Bentivogli, in Bologna; she succeeded in drawing Siena into the League, and, in order to force Genoa to abandon her Florentine alliance, she promised Alfonso ships with which to attack her next year. At the same time she kept up intrigues with the opposition party within Florence, which was occasionally able to hinder the prosecution of Cosimo's projects. Venice even tried to interfere with the privileges of the Florentine traders at Constantinople, "treating us as if we were barbarians and without religion," the Florentines complained; and they retaliated by urging Charles VII. to molest the Venetian merchants in France.

But Venice and Alfonso went still further afield for an ally. The Emperor, Frederick III., had just expressed a determination to visit Italy and be crowned at Rome, and the allies hoped to make capital out of his interference in Italian politics. Frederick, who considered that Milan should have lapsed to the Empire on the failure of the Visconti line, had never granted Sforza's requests for the investiture of the Duchy. He therefore listened to the representations of Sforza's enemies, and gave his adherence to the League of Venice and Alfonso, granting, so it was believed, the investiture of Milan to Alfonso himself. Florence and Sforza were much frightened at his approach, and both attempted to conciliate him. He refused to go to Milan at all, but visited Florence on his way to Rome (January 1452), and was discovered to be a far less awe-inspiring enemy than had been thought. He spent his time bargaining with Florentine merchants for articles of vertu, and watching the fêtes prepared for his amusement. He came accompanied only by a small retinue, and behaved rather as a distinguished foreign visitor than as a Suzerain. He showed himself quite willing to listen to the representations of the Milanese ambassadors on Sforza's behalf, but would make no promises. Yet from Florence and Rome he went on to Naples, and there probably renewed his promises to Alfonso. On the way home he visited Florence again, but she was no longer afraid of him. Not only had he shown himself harmless, but she was now able to count upon a new ally far more powerful, and more likely to interfere actively than he.

Since the summer of 1451, Cosimo and Sforza had been cautiously discussing the advisability of calling for French intervention on their behalf; that is to say, of rousing the cupidity of France by offers of aid for the conquest of Naples for René of Anjou, in return for active help against Venice and Alfonso. It was Visconti who had first set the example of intriguing with France, particularly when, just before his death, he was hard pressed by Venice. His negotiations had probably never been quite in earnest, and still less so were those instituted by Cosimo himself in 1448, with the view of involving Venice in them, and of thus keeping up the enmity between her and Alfonso. In 1451, also, Cosimo's idea was chiefly to frighten the opposition league and the Emperor with threats of the overwhelming power of France, of which power Cosimo and Sforza themselves were not without fear. France, united now, and fast driving out her English invaders, was not to be trifled with; and it was only too plain that the reconquest of Naples for René might but lead to the conquest of Milan for its French claimant, the Duke of Orleans. Therefore when, in September 1451, Agnolo Acciaiuoli was despatched as ambassador to France from Milan and Florence conjointly, his mission was rather to see how the land lay, and to conclude a general alliance, than to make any distinct attempt to call the French into Italy for the present; and he was specially bidden to give no definite promises of aid to a French invading expedition. The plan succeeded well; Acciaiuoli met with a warm reception, and his protestations of the eternal devotion of Florence to the House of France, visibly witnessed by the French lilies which were also the arms of the Republic, were favourably received by Charles VII. Charles was pleased with the idea of extending French influence by re-establishing the Angevins at Naples, and at the same time of employing the troops set free by the close of the English wars, and at present a great embarrassment to him. A preliminary convention was accordingly signed at Montils-les-Tours in April 1452, by which Charles pledged himself to defend Florence or Milan, if either were attacked between that date and the summer of 1453. It was probably the news of this alliance which made the Emperor more complaisant on his second visit to Florence, and at Ferrara, on his way home, he attempted to institute negotiations for a general peace; but Venice and Alfonso had little belief in the practical efficacy of the French alliance. France showed no signs as yet of interfering actively; she was still afraid of another English invasion, and the Duke of Orleans was intriguing at the French Court against Sforza. Accordingly Venice curtly refused the Emperor's offer of mediation, and as soon as he was out of Italy declared war upon Sforza (May 16th, 1452), Alfonso following suit, and declaring war upon Florence (June 11th).

Alfonso had at first intended to borrow ships from Venice, and attack Pisa and Livorno by sea; but after inducing Siena to join the league and grant passage to his troops, he changed his plans and sent his son, Ferrante, to invade Tuscany by land. Ferrante entered the Florentine dominions by way of the Tiber valley, tried, but failed to take Cortona, and then wasted forty-three days in besieging one gallantly-defended fortress, Fojano,—"the martyrdom of Don Ferrante," laughed the Florentines. This long delay enabled Florence to garrison her castles and increase her army; while Ferrante, having crossed the Sienese territory, spent forty-four days more in besieging another small fortress in the Chianti district. Bad weather now set in, and he had to retire to the sea coast in order to receive provisions from Naples. The whole result of his campaign was the capture of Fojano and of an insignificant village called Rencine, and the depredations of his soldiers in the Chianti district. They approached at times very near to Florence, and the citizens, always terrified at the prospect of a siege, were for a time considerably frightened. During the winter, too, Ferrante's ships captured the coast town of Vada, from which starting-point he hoped to attack the Pisan district next year.

Florence was soon tired of war and war-expenses, and throughout the winter the people became very importunate for an accommodation with Alfonso. Sforza never ceased his demands for money, and Florence thought that she had none to spare. Sforza's affairs were not very prosperous; he could not succeed in forcing the Venetian army to a pitched battle, while his rear was harried by Savoy and Montferrat, which Venice had incited to attack him. Agnolo Acciaiuoli had been despatched to France on a second embassy in September 1452, and the first result of his negotiations was that France put pressure on Savoy which forced it to cease its attacks. But Acciaiuoli's mission had this time a further aim. He was to point out to Charles VII. that the moment was favourable for the reconquest of Naples for René; Italy was divided, and France united and powerful as she had never been before; if Charles would come himself, or send a Prince of the Blood with ten or fifteen thousand troops, they, in conjunction with Milan, Florence, and Genoa, could easily recover Naples, which was in a disturbed and discontented condition. If, however, Charles did not wish for the trouble and expense of a Neapolitan expedition, he was to be asked to send French troops into Italy, to be paid by Florence for the defence of herself and of Milan. Cosimo and

Sforza had hesitated long before taking this step, which was a desperate effort to right the Balance of Power, disturbed by the united weight of Venice and Naples; but they were driven to it at last by the apparently implacable enmity of those two allies.

At first Acciaiuoli did not prosper; Charles would do nothing more than negotiate with Savoy; he was in fact distracted by the last efforts of the English at Bordeaux. But in April 1453, Acciaiuoli signed an agreement with René, by which the latter promised to come to Italy himself during the same summer, bringing with him two thousand four hundred horse, for whose services Florence was to pay him ten thousand florins a month.

The news of this arrangement arrived in Florence just at the right moment. A sharp contest was raging in the city about the grants of money demanded by Sforza, and Cosimo's party seemed to be losing the day. Sforza pressed for money on the grounds that "when things go badly here" (in Lombardy), "it is your" (Cosimo's) "loss; and when they go well here, it is your gain." But Cosimo was ill, out of temper, and consequently stingy. Sforza wished that he could himself be three hours with him to convince him of the need of liberal money grants. But Cosimo declared to Nicodemo that he could not see his way to make the Commune grant any favour at present. The Signory and Dieci would be sure to refuse if asked for money, which might lead to a dangerous ill-feeling between Florence and Milan. "Cosimo is in bed," wrote Nicodemo to his master, "and in the hands of a doctor. His illness gives courage to his enemies, so that there is great division and disorder in Florence." The opposition party wanted to obtain peace at once. All the city declared that war could not be continued throughout another summer. A new Dieci of war was about to be elected, and it was very important that its members should be of the Medicean party. Fortunately at this juncture there arrived the news of the compact with René, and it put fresh heart into the Florentines; "they no longer complained of spending or doing what Cosimo wished," and Sforza was promised eighty thousand florins a year. The haggling for money indeed still continued. At one moment Nicodemo, unable to obtain any, declared that "the heart of Pharoah is hardened"; but the scale was really turned in Sforza's favour, as it appeared that René was on the march southwards. He was long on the way, being held in check by Savoy; and Florence wrote urgently, begging him to hasten.

It was not till September that he joined Sforza's camp in the Brescian territory. But the effects of his arrival were immediate and startling. To the last Venice never believed that he would really come, and she was ill prepared. Terrified by the "barbaric" French soldiery, who made war in earnest and not as a game, every town in the Brescian territory but Brescia itself surrendered before the end of the year. Meanwhile in Tuscany, Florence, encouraged by the moral support of her new ally's arrival, had been recovering her losses of last year. Ferrante had lost his best general through illness, and his troops were decimated by sickness and the hardships of the winter in camp. Florence had, on the contrary, obtained from Sforza the services of his brother Alessandro. Rencine and Fojano were recovered in August, and in October, after a long siege, Vada was abandoned by its Neapolitan garrison. Ferrante remained inactive and helpless in the Sienese district; and the war was reduced to recriminatory raids of Florentine and Sienese troops upon one another's territories.

The effect of all these victories was to make Sforza and Cosimo turn to thoughts of peace. It had indeed from the first been their idea to force their enemies to peace by bringing René into Italy and using him against them. Even before René's arrival, Sforza had been in negotiation with Venice; and Florence had, about the same time, assured Sforza that she herself could not continue hostilities beyond the winter, but must speedily seek peace. Yet Acciaiuoli had pledged Florence not to make peace without the consent of Charles VII., and had promised René that, even if she came to terms with Venice, Alfonso should not be included. On René's arrival both Sforza and Florence had been loud in protestations of devotion to his cause, and had led him to understand that, Venice defeated, they would immediately aid him in a campaign against Alfonso. But by this time they were already contemplating a speedy peace. Constantinople had fallen; Venice, it was well known, would be glad to be able to turn all her energies against the Turks. The Pope, also anxious for a united Italy and a crusade, was carrying on negotiations in Rome between the ambassadors of Florence and Naples. Cosimo, however, hoped, by delay and further successes, to obtain better terms, and the negotiations dragged on indefinitely.

Yet Cosimo and Sforza, anxious as they had become for peace, saw plainly the dangers which the sudden dismissal of René without the conquest of Naples might bring upon them. Sforza said, "The matter must be considered very carefully. . . . René has come so far and at so much expense . . . and his coming has been of great reputation to the league . . . it is necessary to manage this affair in such a manner as to satisfy the King of France and René; because, if he thinks we do not esteem and value him sufficiently, he will be angry with us, and will stir up the anger of the King of France against us, and the French nation will become our enemy, which will be very bad for Florence, and more particularly for us who are near to them" (Sforza is thinking of the Orleans claim to Milan) . . . "so we must carry ourselves very prudently in the said affair in order to keep the" (friendship of the) "House of France."

René had at first been taken in by their protestations, had even tried to negotiate with Venice for Sforza; but at last he began to fathom the designs of his allies, and to understand that, when Florence wrote that "his aid had enabled them to gain either a definite victory, or an advantageous and honourable peace," it was really the peace of which she was thinking. He made the discovery too soon for his allies, who had intended to use him to frighten their enemies still further, and who were far from pleased when, at the end of the year, he suddenly announced his intention of returning immediately to France. Sforza and Cosimo made every effort to induce him to stay, but René was obdurate, and all that could be got from him was a promise to send his son Jean, titular Duke of Calabria, to take military service with Florence. There was no open breach; protestations of eternal friendship passed on both sides; but in reality there was a complete break between René and Sforza, neither of whom ever forgave the other for his disappointment. So secret had been the whole transaction that in Italy it was generally believed that René had gone home out of mere fickleness; but that chronicler understood the situation who wrote, "The design of René was to make a peace between Milan and Venice, and then with Sforza's help to invade Naples; but it turned out to the contrary, for Sforza made use of his reputation to terrify the Venetians, and made peace for himself; and thus King René, having exalted Duke Francesco, was tricked by him and went again to France."

The result of René's retirement was to hasten the inevitable peace. Sforza and Cosimo were now ready to agree to any reasonable terms; Sforza wanted quiet to enable him to establish himself at Milan; Venice to concentrate herself on her Eastern affairs; Florence had spent money freely and needed to recuperate her finances. Cosimo sent pressing messages to Sforza to hasten negotiations; but he was also anxious that Castiglione and its neighbourhood should be recovered from Alfonso by the terms of the treaty, in order that Florence might at least not be said to have lost territorially by the war. The other Italian powers were, however, taken by surprise when, in March 1454, Venice and Sforza announced that they had concluded a treaty with one another, reserving places in it for their allies as adherents. Florence and Alfonso were naturally far from pleased at finding their hands forced in this manner; Alfonso refused point-blank to ratify: Cosimo hesitated, but finally gave way to Sforza's representations, and to the public feeling of Florence, where the need for rest and for a diminution of taxation were painfully felt. "The citizens of Florence," wrote the Venetian ambassador, "have raised a great outcry over the new taxes, and sharp words are said against Cosimo and others who wish for war. Two hundred families . . . are in very bad circumstances, and have to sell their property to pay the taxes. Cosimo, in order not to lose the favour of the people, has many bushels of corn distributed every day amongst the poor, who murmur loudly against the dearness of provisions."

The Peace of Lodi was published on April 11th, and was confirmed by all the Italian states except Alfonso and Genoa, the latter afraid of being forced to pay tribute to Alfonso again if she ratified it. In the autumn the Peace was converted into a League for twenty-five years, which the Pope hoped might lead to a crusade of united Italy. But no one could feel secure until Alfonso had been included in it, and the difficulties of including him were great on all accounts. Alfonso needed to be propitiated for the slighting manner in which he had been treated; and even then, so long as Sforza and Florence held to their French alliance, he felt that they were still threatening him with René of Anjou, and he could not with dignity or safety become their ally.

But it was not easy for Florence to relinquish her alliance with the French, and impossible to do so without mortally offending them. Charles VII. had been much less angry than might have been expected at her treatment of René, had seemed inclined to throw the blame on René rather than on Florence and Sforza, and to have believed Sforza's assurances that the complaints which René made against him were "not honest, nor just, nor true, but frivolous and light and without any substantial foundation." But to openly repudiate Charles's alliance must bring his wrath upon Florence; and, even if Cosimo had dared risk it, his fellow-citizens were far too much attached to their traditional friendship with France, and the mercantile privileges which it ensured them, to surrender it for any consideration. The Florentine populace were ready to assert that Milan and Venice wished to disarm and render them powerless by making them abandon the French alliance. The position was further complicated by the actual presence of Jean, titular Duke of Calabria, in Florence, in pursuance of the arrangement made between the Republic and René when the latter quitted Italy.

Cosimo had to carry through the negotiations with diplomatic subtlety. On the one hand, Alfonso was assured that the French League was practically abandoned, and that the Duke of Calabria would soon have to be dismissed for want of funds to pay his stipend. On the other hand, Jean was assured that Florence was only forced by necessity to bow to the immediate circumstances, and that the peace with Alfonso would be but a temporary measure to enable her to recover from her financial embarrassments. Both parties were successfully managed; the Duke of Calabria was actually persuaded to give his consent to peace between Florence and Alfonso; in January 1455 Alfonso joined the Italian League, only stipulating that

Genoa should not be included in it; and it was publicly proclaimed all over Italy on March 25th.

It was many years since Florence had enjoyed a peace so firm and so lasting as that inaugurated by the Treaty of Lodi. The rest which it brought was badly needed for her financial recuperation; the resumption of the interrupted commerce with Venice and Naples, and the safety of her Oriental trading vessels from attack by the Venetian and Aragonese navies gave a powerful impulse to the commercial prosperity on which her very existence depended, while the cessation of war-taxation was felt a great relief at home. She had made no territorial increase by the last war; yet to all the more thoughtful citizens it must have seemed that her substantial gains outweighed her financial sacrifices. She had greatly increased her importance amongst the Italian states; instead of being the mere ally and dependent of Venice, she had shown that she could stand alone, apart from Venice, even head a counter league. Of Venice and Alfonso she was no longer afraid. As a barrier to protect her against the one, she had established Sforza at Milan, devoted by common interests to her service; against the other she could count on a still more powerful ally, France. The league with France had given her no small reputation in Italy, where, as Sforza said, "war is waged chiefly by reputation."

All this was due to Cosimo and Cosimo's policy. He had often been obliged to force Florence to act as he wished in the teeth of the most violent opposition; yet he had at last led her to support him, and had enabled her to assume her new and commanding position. Yet

Cosimo himself was even more than the ruler of one amongst the Italian states; his was virtually the master-mind which had evolved the political conditions of 1454 out of those of 1441. Sforza and Venice had long ago discovered that Cosimo's was the chief personality with which they had to deal, and that they could never obtain their own ends without either cajoling or frightening him, while Venice had discovered to her cost that he was not easily frightened. For the future also, what Cosimo did and what Cosimo wished was to be of supreme importance in Italian affairs. So carefully too had he acted that, in spite of the opposition party within Florence, by means of which Venice had tried to work against him, he had at last succeeded in identifying the policy and interests of the Republic with his own. The other Powers had learnt their lesson, and knew that whatever was desired from Florence must be obtained through Cosimo only, and by no other means. There was no longer any chance that the Republic, though still sometimes hanging back, would ever again try to act independently of him.

What Cosimo had in fact done was to realise the theory of a Balance of Powers. The Italian states, after the conquest of Milan by Sforza, had fallen into two natural parties, the claimants of Milan against its *de facto* lord; Cosimo, by allying himself with the latter, had made the Leagues almost equal, and, when his opponents seemed the stronger, he had, by calling in the French, redressed the balance.

For the last ten years of his life, his aim was to maintain the balance which had been thus established. But for the future Cosimo hoped to maintain it without involving Florence in war. Florence needed that the peace which he had given her should be more than a truce, and Cosimo himself was growing old, and felt more confidence in the efforts of his diplomacy than in his power to carry through another war. Since Florence therefore no longer took part in the wars of Italy, her place in the politics seems less marked; yet Cosimo was never really more influential than in the last few years of his life. Still, in the future, as in the past, the main line of his policy was the maintenance of the Milanese alliance, in which he felt that his own strength lay. The tie which bound him to Sforza was never loosened, although Cosimo expressed disappointment that Sforza had never done anything personally for him, —never for instance made any attempt to obtain Lucca. But he still remained, as Nicodemo expressed it to Sforza himself, "your faithful friend and servant; since he held you to be his god in this world, which I would not say, if I had not often heard him say it himself." Though their alliance was based on common interests, Cosimo was the least self-seeking of the two; Sforza, in spite of his many protestations, was often frankly selfish; but Cosimo might say with truth to Nicodemo, "I have passed through troubles and borne great dangers sometimes in order to gain the friendship of your lord the duke."

The conditions of Italian politics were, from 1454 onwards, somewhat altered by the practical withdrawal of Venice, which was absorbed henceforth in her Oriental affairs. Yet since France, through her alliance with Florence, now virtually took rank as an Italian Power, the number of factors to be dealt with in the political problem was not decreased. The first movement was the rapid drawing together of Alfonso and Sforza, whose interests, now that Alfonso had relinquished his designs on Milan, really lay together, since the secure tenure by each of his dominions was more or less definitely threatened by the growing strength of France. Alfonso was afraid of René of Anjou, Sforza of the Duke of Orleans. A marriage-treaty was concluded between them in the autumn of 1455, by which a daughter and son of Sforza were betrothed to a grandson and granddaughter of Alfonso. Cosimo's aim was to act a mediatory part between them and France, and so ward off danger of war.

When they summoned the French into Italy, Sforza and Cosimo had in fact conjured up a Frankenstein which was speedily becoming unmanageable. They had themselves been afraid of the result of their own action, and had hesitated long before finally inviting René's expedition. For the French, having discovered the delights of Italy, and how little the Italians were capable of defending their own country for themselves, could never henceforth be contented without intriguing amongst the Italian states to obtain opportunities for invasion and conquest. This pleased Cosimo as little as it did Sforza; since the French established at either end of the Peninsula, in Naples or in Milan, would, by their superior strength, utterly upset his carefully arranged Balance of the Powers.

Alfonso himself was the first difficulty that Cosimo and Sforza had to deal with. Alfonso proved very troublesome even after he joined the League; he sought a personal revenge on Siena for joining it before himself, and so forcing him to withdraw Ferrante from Tuscany sooner than he had wished; for this purpose he secretly prompted the Condottiere, Jacopo Piccinino, just dismissed from the service of Venice, to quarter his army on the Sienese territory, and commit serious devastations there. Piccinino was driven to Naples by the united forces of the North-Italian states and the Pope, Calixtus III., who succeeded Nicolas V. in 1455; but so serious had been the condition of things that the Pope had threatened to call in a French army to suppress Piccinino. Sforza's terror at the bare idea shows how far he was from wishing for another French invasion; he exhorted Alfonso to conciliate the Pope, even at the sacrifice of something of his own dignity, and to give up Piccinino and his revenge on Siena, rather than bring upon Italy the storm of a French invasion. Again, he remonstrated with Alfonso on account of his determined hostility to Genoa, which had been excepted from the League to please him, as likely to drive Genoa into the arms of France. Alfonso was less afraid of the French; "they are men of talk, but not of deeds," he said; but what Sforza feared was precisely what did happen. The Duke of Calabria, leaving Florence at the end of his prescribed period of service, with many expressions of friendship and devotion on both sides, was called to their aid by the Genoese, rendered desperate by Alfonso's attacks. He took possession of the town in the name of Charles VII., administering its affairs himself as Lieutenant-Governor under France, and thus gave the French a stable footing in Italy. Alfonso's last attack upon Genoa was defeated, and Alfonso himself died almost immediately afterwards.

His death made a considerable change in Italian politics. His successor, Ferrante, had far less political insight and energy; he needed rather to be propped up at Naples than to be allowed to maintain himself there. At the same time he had less of that restless ambition which had made his father the chief element of disturbance in Italy. Pope Calixtus, however, complicated affairs by refusing to invest Ferrante with the Neapolitan kingdom, and declaring it lapsed to the Holy See, intending to bestow it upon his own worthless Borgia nephews, and giving up the project of a crusade, for which he had been most eager, in order to gratify this ambition. Sforza, as the ally of Alfonso, protected his son, Ferrante, feeling indeed that the son would be a less troublesome ally than the father, because more dependent upon himself. The Duke of Calabria thought the moment favourable for making offers to Sforza to restore to him the lands which he had once held in the Neapolitan kingdom in return for help to overthrow Ferrante; but Sforza refused the offer, and even secretly aided some Genoese rebels against the French. Sforza declared to Cosimo that he preferred to have at Naples Ferrante, "who has become altogether an Italian," rather than "the proud and insolent French, who are full of contempt for Italian customs, and who are already too influential in Italy."

All depended upon the attitude that Cosimo and Florence would adopt. In the city the feeling in favour of the Angevins was strong. The French alliance had been found too valuable in the past to be lightly forfeited, while the citizens still bore a natural grudge against the House of Aragon for the two recent invasions of Tuscany. The taking of Genoa by the French had been hailed with joy; the death of Alfonso was considered "good news" in Florence, "because of the constant trouble he had given the city, for indeed his whole life had been spent in giving trouble to others." Ferrante contrived to give offence by interfering with some Florentine ships; and the people declared they would rather "give themselves over to the Grand Turk than suffer such an insult." For a short time Cosimo allowed himself to be led away by the popular sentiments; he feared to endanger the French alliance; he believed that Ferrante's cause was hopeless, and that he was no better than "a dead man." He urged Sforza to yield to circumstances, and offered to make a good bargain for him with France. For once Sforza refused to be led by him, remaining firm in the conviction that the French should not be admitted farther into Italy; and he soon succeeded in persuading Cosimo to revert to his opinion. Accordingly, on the accession of a new Pope, Pius II., Sforza and Cosimo contrived, by working on his well-known desire for a crusade, to persuade him that the only way to secure peace in Italy, and make a crusade possible, was to grant the investiture of Naples to Ferrante. This was accordingly done in the autumn of 1458. Cosimo was not the man who, once he had embraced a particular line of policy, would shrink from carrying it out, but his difficulties on this occasion were considerable. Not only would it have been a Herculean task to induce the Florentines to abandon the French alliance and actively embrace the cause of Ferrante, but it was not the course which Cosimo himself desired. To maintain the French alliance nominally, so that it might be renewed when more favourable circumstances should permit, while acting with apparent neutrality, was the policy to which he persuaded his fellow-citizens. It was easy to work upon them so far, in spite of their personal attachment to the Duke of Calabria and their trust in France, by pointing out that only thus could Florence preserve the peace which was proving so advantageous, and retain her commercial relations with both France and Naples. Accordingly, when envoys from both parties arrived in the winter of 1458, and pressed for open support and assistance, Florence refused to commit herself to either, excusing herself to France on the grounds that she could not violate the Peace of 1455, to Ferrante that she was bound by private ties to France.

To this policy Florence publicly adhered throughout the invasion of Naples by the Duke of Calabria, which was begun in the autumn of 1459, and ended with the final victory of Ferrante in 1463; but Cosimo's private policy went beyond, or rather behind, this. He still contrived to provide Sforza with money, which practically meant providing Ferrante, since it went to pay the troops which Sforza despatched to Ferrante's aid, or to help the Genoese exiles against the French. Cosimo too helped to keep the Pope steady to the cause. Still bent on a crusade, Pius called a Congress of the European Powers together at Mantua in 1459, and on his way thither visited Florence, where he was met by young Galeazzo, Sforza's eldest son, and elaborate fêtes were devised in their honour. Then, no doubt, Cosimo and Pius discussed what was best to be done for Ferrante. At Mantua Sforza himself was present, and persuaded the Pope not to heed the angry protests of the French ambassadors, their demands for René's investiture of Naples and the abandonment of Ferrante, and their appeals to a future Council. But when the news of the Duke of Calabria's actual invasion of Naples reached Mantua, it was no longer necessary to stimulate the Pope's wrath artificially. War in Naples meant the ruin of his crusading plan, the Congress had to be abandoned, and the Pope went home to concert measures in Ferrante's favour, once more visiting Florence on the way (January 1460), when doubtless he and Cosimo again pledged each other to support Ferrante. Shortly afterwards the French ambassadors at Mantua visited Florence, and succeeded in extracting from the Signory a promise of 80,000 florins for the Duke of Calabria; but Cosimo persuaded them to annul the grant, and to declare their neutrality again in somewhat "sharp terms."

At first things went ill with Ferrante; he was deserted and defeated by his general, Piccinino; the Papal and Milanese troops were driven from the country; but Sforza was able to change the face of affairs by a counter-blow, the rebellion of Genoa from the French (March 1461). This loss cut the Angevins in Naples off from their easy communications with France, and from this moment the fortune of the war began to turn in Ferrante's favour. Sforza had, in fact, a secret alliance with the Dauphin Louis, who was as usual acting in opposition to his own father, and this gave him courage to face the wrath of France. Almost immediately afterwards, however, Charles VII. died, and the Dauphin became King Louis XI.

Louis was no sooner on the throne than he changed

his views, adopted the traditional policy of France and of his father, and warmly embraced the Angevin cause. He suggested a marriage between the Royal House and that of Anjou, and, throwing over his alliance with Sforza, declared his intention of punishing him for his part in the rebellion of Genoa. Through his many intrigues in Italy, Louis was fully acquainted with Italian affairs, and was possessed of an almost more than Italian political cunning,—"he might have lived and have been brought up in Italy," said Sforza's ambassador. His ambition was to obtain influence in Italy by any means which he found convenient, and the cause of the Angevins was the first instrument which lay ready to his hand. Soon, however, he found that he was more likely to succeed in Italy by diplomacy than by force; for embassies from every part of Italy poured in upon him, and he made excellent use of the opportunities for interference which they offered him. Amongst them was an embassy from Florence, and Louis, who well understood the value of the Florentine alliance to the Angevins, laid himself out to be specially condescending, and to heap marks of his favour upon the ambassadors. His plan was to make use of Cosimo (since he knew, as Nicodemo wrote to Sforza, that "Cosimo can do what he wills with your Highness"), in order to detach Sforza from his league with Ferrante, and to make him return to his old alliance with France. He declared to the Florentine ambassadors that he was "Sforza's intimate and peculiar friend"; he made the most tempting offers to Sforza—protection from the Orleans claim, and a marriage into the Angevin family for his daughter, who was still betrothed to Ferrante's son. Then Louis persuaded the Florentine ambassadors to accompany his own embassy to Milan, and aid with their exhortations in the separation of Sforza from Ferrante. Sforza's position was difficult; Ferrante was still in great danger; the Pope, coaxed and threatened in turn by Louis, was wavering; Sforza himself was ill, and his own dominions were in disorder. In this juncture, however, he was encouraged by an embassy from Florence, sent by Cosimo to give him the moral support of its presence in his difficulties. Cosimo, in fact, was not to be made use of as an intermediary so easily as Louis fancied. He was now quite of Sforza's opinion that the French were not to be tolerated at Naples. To establish them there would be to render them overwhelmingly powerful, and to upset the Balance of Power which had been so carefully adjusted. To pacify Louis and to gain time, he allowed sham negotiations between France and Sforza to be carried on in his name at Florence, negotiations which were also intended to disarm the suspicions of his own fellow-citizens, who were beginning to be afraid that, unless they broke with Sforza, his obstinacy would draw down the wrath of France upon them also. Sforza was demanding 50,000 ducats early in 1462; the Florentines refused to grant it, "because they thought that they were going to be led into a war with France to the ruin of their trade."

Yet it was not until they were sure that the campaign of the Duke of Calabria in Naples was a hopeless failure that Cosimo and Sforza would listen seriously to Louis's persuasions. Then, when the Angevins were no longer dangerous, genuine negotiations began, Cosimo acting as intermediary between France and Sforza. In May 1463 an alliance was concluded, which led, later in the year, to an agreement by which the French rights on Genoa and Savona were ceded to Sforza, and he obtained possession of those towns early in 1464. Louis was, in fact, beginning to find himself in difficulties at home, and he wanted to be able to count on Sforza's friendship. He cared no longer for the interests of the Angevins, since they were opposing his domestic policy. Cosimo felt safe from French interference when Louis was thus occupied within France. It seemed to him that "all is over with the prospects of the House of Anjou in Italy." The French alliance would be no longer a danger, but would once more "lend its reputation" to Sforza and to Florence. The fears of the Florentines being removed by the new League, there was great joy in the city over Sforza's success at Genoa. The 50,000 ducats were voted to him; the citizens thronged to Nicodemo's house to congratulate,—"it seemed to them as if they had got Genoa themselves, since they considered all Sforza's exaltation to yield them peace and prosperity." Cosimo said "that now God might do what he willed with his life, for he should depart contented."

In forwarding a French and Milanese alliance Cosimo had another end in view, namely, to put a check upon a possible *rapprochement* between Milan and Venice. He still distrusted and disliked Venice: "Nicodemo," he said, "did you ever know more bare-faced liars than the Venetians are?" He believed that, under pretence of arranging for a crusade in company with Sforza, they had been intriguing to separate Milan from Florence.

Florence had no desire for crusades. She found her eastern trade went on very well, though the Turks were at Constantinople, and she more than half suspected all the crusade agitation, in the name of religion, to be a mere trick of the Venetians to extend their own influence in the Levant, which Florence on the contrary had little objection to seeing limited by the Turks. Up to the last hour of his life Cosimo was harried by the crusade question, by the complaints of Venice to Louis XI. that Florence was actually aiding the Turks with ships, and by what seemed to him the singularly ill-judged energy of Pius II. in setting off for the crusade in person.

To the last Cosimo had hopes that Sforza, now at the zenith of his power, would exert himself to procure Lucca for his friend, "to offer as the best gift of his rule to the Florentines"; but Sforza no doubt decided that he would not embroil Italy anew for an old man's fancy. And, with or without Lucca, Cosimo might fairly consider his foreign policy to have been a success. The territorial gains were small,—great states were not to be won and lost in the fifteenth century as they were in the fourteenth,—but the increase in the importance, the "reputation" of Florence was enormous. A most powerful ally had been created for her in Lombardy; the French, while prevented from making any permanent acquisitions in the Peninsula, had yet been employed with skill and daring to strengthen the position of the Republic. Florence had been made the balancing, the mediating force in Italy, and thus had obtained a certain independence, which yet was not isolation. Cosimo had encountered and surmounted the preliminary difficulties of this line of policy. His grandson, Lorenzo, was able, with far more ease and still greater success, to make use of Florence in the same manner, and enable her to fill still more effectively the same part in Italian politics. In one sense Cosimo seemed to hold himself aloof from his Italian contemporaries. He was not agitated to the same extent by their personal fears and ambitions, and thus he was able to establish himself like an arbiter above them.

It is in Cosimo's foreign policy, almost more than in any other department of his rule, that he establishes his claim to be the earliest of modern statesmen, since it was he who, by means of a thoroughly modern diplomacy, made the Balance of Power into a practical working system. For it was that diplomacy of finesse, of intrigue, of combining and shifting alliances with Machiavellian skill and cunning, and with less than Machiavellian morality, which formed the delicate machinery by which it was possible to adjust and maintain the Balance of Power.

CHAPTER V

THE DOMESTIC POLICY OF COSIMO DE' MEDICI AND THE CONSOLIDATION OF HIS POWER

HITHERTO, in tracing the course of Cosimo's life and domestic policy, he has seemed to the dispassionate observer to have been rather acted upon than acting on his own initiative. His family name, his wealth, and known abilities caused him to be put forward as the representative of a party in need of a leader to give it cohesion, and to be seized upon by the opposing party as a convenient scapegoat to suffer as an example to the rest. In reality Cosimo was waiting his time patiently, laying the foundations of his future influence by means of his wealth and liberality, trusting to the violence of his enemies and the growing strength of his friends to do the rest, preferring to be restored to Florence and set up on a pinnacle as the hero-martyr of the late Government than to make his own way back by the force of his individual efforts, so that it was not he but his adherents who should seem responsible for the violence of the revolution. Yet during the years immediately after his restoration, he contrived so to draw his party about him, to identify it so closely with himself and its interests with his, that its very existence was involved in his safety, and for the future it would have to stand or fall according to his fortunes.

He began at once to form a regular system of policy; it was partly destructive, partly constructive, and it was based on the experience which he had acquired from the mistakes and weaknesses of his enemies.

The chief points in which they had erred were three. First, in allowing the permanence and incrustation of an elaborate system of class distinctions. This was a defect inherent in the character of an oligarchy, which, forming an exclusive class in itself, tended to make the other classes exclusive and separated by hard and fast lines from one another. The Major and Minor Arts were rigidly distinguished; it was almost impossible to move from one to the other. Equally difficult was it for one of the Grandi to enter the ranks of the Popolani. All these classes were still more differentiated by the varying measures of political power accorded to them; while the lowest class of all was as distinctly cut off by its total exclusion from politics.

Cosimo, like all rulers who wish to be absolute, made it his aim to equalise as far as possible those whom he hoped to make his subjects. It was his object to break up the solidarity of classes, and destroy that strong class feeling which was so powerful an incentive to discontent and disturbance. For this purpose he would have obliterated the distinction between Grandi and Popolani altogether, but that the existence of a Grandi class was too convenient for the purpose of political proscription. So that, instead of following Rinaldo's example of extending the rights of the Popolani to the Grandi, he pursued the opposite method of converting nearly all the Grandi into Popolani, at the same time taking from those Grandi who remained—mostly members of the Albizzi party, lately proscribed—their peculiar rights to certain offices. The class as a class was broken up, while the newly made Popolani were wholly dependent on himself to enable them to pass the Scrutinies and obtain the ordinary offices.

On the other hand, the distinction between Major and Minor Arts was blurred and rendered indistinct by the elevation of the Pucci and other wealthy persons from the Minor to the Major. This weakened the Major by destroying their exclusiveness, while it weakened the Minor by depriving them of their principal members. And Cosimo made a regular system of the employment of "new men"—in this respect also like other rulers who wish to become tyrants, including our own Henry VIII. They were used as a means to depress the older families which had hitherto enjoyed a monopoly of government, and to supply the places left vacant by the exiles: "Two yards of red cloth," Cosimo said, "are enough to make a citizen." These "new men," dependent entirely on his favour for advancement, were ready to carry out his policy with docility under his directions. Cosimo had the gift of choosing men well, and those whom he selected were capable, if unscrupulous. They made him independent of the upper classes for officials, and, possessing an hereditary hatred against those who had so long oppressed them, they were willing to execute any scheme for the suppression of Cosimo's rivals. At the same time the possibilities of advancement which he first opened to them made him very popular with the lower classes, whom it was always his object to conciliate.

Secondly, the Albizzi government was weak because it had lost its control over the distribution of taxation. The Catasto was, however, so lately established and so popular that the Mediceans were afraid to meddle with it openly, or even at first to disregard it. But new Registers ought to have been made in 1434 and 1437 to mark the changes in the distribution of property, and this was neglected; so that many Mediceans whose wealth had been steadily increasing since 1431 had no corresponding increase in their quota of taxation.

But it was Cosimo's first and chief care to obtain and keep that hold over the official government, the want of which was the immediate cause of the Albizzi's fall. The danger of this want of control showed itself in two ways:—in the weak, uncertain action of the official government in times of external difficulty, when a strong hand was needed, and in the very different activity and rapidity which it could display in carrying through a domestic revolution when backed by a powerful party in opposition. The first defect Cosimo was not in a position to remedy for the present; his hold upon the government was not yet strong enough; he was obliged to work as he could through or in the Dieci and Signory. In 1440 we find the executive almost as incompetent, and quite as easily panic-stricken as it had been in 1430. But the second danger Cosimo avoided by reducing the official government to a position of dependence upon himself far more complete than anything the Albizzi had ever contemplated. In order not to infringe more than was necessary upon the constitutional forms and theoretical liberties to which the Florentines were so much attached, no definite function was formally taken from any office or council supposed to possess it; powers which it was inconvenient to allow them to exercise were declared "suspended," not "annulled." There was no diminution in the outward importance and dignity of the offices; control over them was simply obtained by controlling the selection of the officials. The short terms of office rendered it easy to punish the officials thus selected for any attempts at independence while in office; the only necessity was to retain the actual appointment in trustworthy hands. One of the principal tasks of the Balìa which had restored Cosimo from exile was to make new Scrutinies for all the offices, internal and external. There was no question this time of letting names already in the Borse remain there as the Albizzi had done; a thorough clearance of all doubtful names was effected. Yet however safe the Scrutiny might be, if selection of the Signory by lot from the Borse were retained, it was possible that a man whose politics had changed, or who had some recent cause for discontent, might yet slip into office. But the Balìa avoided this danger by appointing a sub-committee of Accopiatori, whose power was to last on after its own should have lapsed, and was only to cease at the end of five years instead of at the end of one, as had been the case with the Accopiatori of 1433. Their work was to choose every two months a Signory from amongst the names already scrutinised and put in the Borse. Thus any one even suspected of unsoundness could be effectually excluded from the Signory.

"Warned by the ruin of their opponents," says

Machiavelli, "they judged that a scrutiny alone was not sufficient, and therefore appointed Accopiatori." These Accopiatori were of course very powerful. One contemporary calls them "the ten tyrants." It was Cosimo's personal work to keep them well in hand, to take care that all their appointments were made at his own command, and that they should not gain a position independent of himself. It is a proof of how well he accomplished this that he found it feasible to have almost the same persons appointed as Accopiatori again and again throughout his lifetime.

The functions of the Balìa were not, however, limited to these; it passed many important measures while still sitting during the months after Cosimo's return. On its authority the Grandi were made Popolani, and members of the Minor raised to the Major Arts. Another use which Cosimo made of it was to bring the control of superior criminal justice into the hands of his own party, a matter of great importance in the disturbed state of the city. The Podestà, who had hitherto been the chief criminal judge, had of late lost much of his reputation. Though a foreigner he could not be depended upon for impartiality, nor even for always acting as the interests of the ruling party dictated. In 1435 the Podestà dared commute a death-sentence on some of the rebels to imprisonment for life. Angry at this sign of independence the Balìa dismissed him. "Here was to be seen," exclaimed a contemporary, "the beginning of tyranny in Florence!" For the future the Balìa determined to supersede the Podestà in all criminal matters affecting the State by the magistracy called the "Otto di Balìa," or "di Guardia," which had hitherto been appointed occasionally, and in 1433 had been given great powers, but which was now made still more powerful, and during Cosimo's lifetime gradually became permanent, and formed the supreme court of criminal jurisdiction. Its members were carefully selected by the Balìa, so that it was really a tribunal of the ruling party itself to sit in judgment on its own enemies. "They decided," says Machiavelli, "that all magistrates who had power over life and death ought to be of their party, and therefore they gave these powers to the Otto di Guardia." The Otto thus became, like the office of the Accopiatori in another department of State, a kind of permanent sub-committee of the Balìa, to whom the Balìa deputed its powers on the expiration of its own authority. Thus the work of proscription left unfinished by the Balìa was completed by the Otto.

For though the Albizzi and their chief partisans had been driven out of Florence, and most of the rest made incapable of office, the work of consolidating the new government was as yet far from complete. The Albizzi were not without friends in the city who would risk something for them, and abroad they counted on the help of Visconti, who found the close alliance between Cosimo and Venice the greatest check on his ambitions. In the first few years of Cosimo's rule there was a constant succession of attempts on the part of the fallen oligarchs from within and without to recover their lost position. All through 1435 and 1436 plots and proscriptions continued; fresh sentences of exile and of political disability were passed,—"A city ruined is better than a city lost," was Cosimo's answer to complaints of the harm done to the Republic by the loss of so many eminent citizens. The possessions of those who had broken their bounds and been declared rebels were forfeited; writing to or receiving letters from exiles was forbidden; exiles who had finished their terms of banishment were yet not allowed to return home unless they received thirty-four favourable votes out of the thirty-seven in the Signory and Colleges.

The Milanese invasions, undertaken at the suggestion of Albizzi, and accompanied by him and other exiles, have already been described.[1] The most serious of these was that of Piccinino in 1440, when the Milanese army and the exiles marched almost unhindered up the Mugello and threatened Florence itself. As they approached the city the panic within was very great. The Contadini, pouring in from the Mugello, gave accounts of the strength of Piccinino's army, and increased the general confusion by encamping with their families and flocks in the narrow streets of the town. When provisions began to run short, and it was feared that Piccinino would cut off the lower Arno and the food supplies which came thence from the city, the Government seemed paralysed. Its members met in the Palace and talked, but appeared to do nothing. Many of them, instead of assisting in improving the defences of the town, collected all the men-at-arms that they could into their private houses, as if expecting an internal revolution. It was long since the citizens themselves had carried arms in open warfare, and the number of troops available for the defence of the city was very small. Neri Capponi was the only person who showed any pluck. He gathered a few soldiers, and making a sally

[1] See Chapter III.

from the gates recovered from Piccinino's garrison the neighbouring village of Remole. Even Cosimo seems for the moment to have lost his head. He offered to go into voluntary exile that the city might not suffer on his account. This may have been merely a bid for popularity; but Neri Capponi must have thought Cosimo really in danger, since he gave directions to one of the Condottieri captains to reserve a hundred soldiers for Cosimo's personal protection if Florence was captured.

But after all there was no sign of a revolt within. Cosimo was much more popular amongst the people than were the Albizzi; and even to those who preferred the latter, the entrance of Piccinino's foreign force within the walls of the city, and a possible sack, seemed too high a price to pay for their restoration.

With the battle of Anghiari and the subsequent peace all serious danger from the rebels was at an end. It had been proved to them and to Visconti that, even under severe pressure, the Florentines would not rise in their favour. On the walls of the Palace of the Signory effigies of those who had borne arms against the Republic were painted, after the rude fashion of the time, hanging by the heels, with insulting verses affixed to each portrait. All that was left to the exiles was to bear their banishment as patiently as they could, and those who had offended least might hope for ultimate restoration to their homes. Rinaldo himself made a pilgrimage to the Holy Land, and returned to Italy only to die suddenly in 1442.

Free from the pressure of external danger, Cosimo could now turn his attention to enlarging the sphere of his authority within Florence. It was his aim to found a dynastic power; and now that he was himself tolerably secure he could look forward to future events, and choose with deliberate purpose the directions in which he intended to extend his influence and the means of so doing. It was in view of these dynastic ambitions that he embarked upon the independent and constructive foreign policy of which the Peace of Lodi formed the culminating point. But to carry through a policy like this Cosimo had need of more than the ill-planned machinery by which foreign affairs had hitherto been managed. He had to be his own "Foreign Minister," and supersede, by direct relations between himself and foreign Powers, the clumsy, old-fashioned methods of acting through the Signory and Dieci. It is true that the ambassadors were still nominally appointed by one or other of these bodies, and still continued to direct official correspondence and make reports to them; but it was Cosimo by whom they were really commissioned and to whom they were really responsible. On one occasion we find him deliberately cancelling the appointment of two ambassadors to Venice, and providing that Neri Capponi should go in their place; on another he recalled his son Piero from an embassy to Venice, and Piero's fellow-ambassadors felt obliged, though much against their will, to follow him home. The ambassadors corresponded privately with Cosimo, and were entrusted by him with much diplomatic business of which the Dieci knew nothing. We hear of Dietisalvi Neroni and Bernadetto de' Medici, on their return from a mission to Milan, first of all explaining to Cosimo all that they had accomplished, and from him receiving instructions how much they were to impart to the Signory and how much to withhold.

At the same time he established private relations between himself and some of the foreign rulers with whom he had to deal, and especially with Sforza, who carried on a long and intimate correspondence with him. Of great assistance to him in this respect were the banking houses of the Medici firm, already established everywhere in Italy and in some foreign towns, and usually in close relations with the various governments upon financial matters. The failure of the effort made by Venice to ignore the fact that Cosimo was absolute "Minister for External Affairs," and to treat directly with the Signory, has already been narrated. All the Powers learned that they had to instruct their ambassadors as Sforza instructed his: "Go to Florence and have an interview with Cosimo; and then, if Cosimo thinks well, present yourself to the Signory. Tell the Signory more or less of your commission as Cosimo thinks good."

Such a complete appropriation of power was not gained without a struggle. Cosimo's foreign policy was warmly opposed, not only by the ignorant, but by men otherwise of his own party, like Neri Capponi; and even a professed Medicean like Agnolo Acciaiuoli hesitated before embracing it. Cosimo had to trust entirely to his personal influence over such men to persuade them to let him have his own way. There was no regular Ministry for Foreign Affairs of which he could get control, but he held one official position which really helped him, his post as an "officer of the Monte," which he retained all through his lifetime. The Monte

Commune of Florence corresponded roughly with our National Debt. All money lent to the Government was said to be " written on the Monte," that is to say, considered part of the National Debt, and it received interest out of the public funds. But as the regular income of the State was very small, and in war time the extra expenses had to be met by demanding forced loans, the greater part of the financial business of the Commune passed through the hands of the Monte officials. After 1441, these officials were elected by the Government, and no longer chosen by lot as heretofore. Cosimo was one of them himself, and was very careful in the selection of the others. On the death of his son Giovanni, for example, Cosimo filled his place upon the Monte with young Pandolfo Pandolfini, who had just shown himself worthy of high trust.

The use which Cosimo made of his position on the Monte can be shown by one example. He had privately lent Sforza thirty thousand florins, and the Councils refused to vote a tax to repay him. Then Cosimo had a law passed, "more to be feared than desired," and "full of cruelty," giving power to the officials of the Monte to enforce the payment of all debts due to the Commune, whether they had already been compounded for or no, and thus obtaining the thirty thousand florins with which to repay himself what he had given Sforza. Is it to be wondered at that Cosimo was popularly accused of having all the "Casse" (collecting-boxes of the Customs officials) emptied at his own house, and that in 1446 he had the greatest difficulty in procuring his own re-election on the Monte, although the electors were all supposed to be of his party? But the importance in which Cosimo held this office is shown by the vigorous and successful efforts which he made to secure it upon this occasion.

For a new and ambitious foreign policy and the wars that it involved much money was necessary, and the Catasto, as already constituted, was not a satisfactory means of procuring it. The people with whom the Catasto was popular were the opposition, for whom it ensured equality of taxation, and the poorer classes. Cosimo had no wish that the former should escape, and could take care of the latter by other means. To the wealthy merchants, who formed the most influential section of his own party, the Catasto was detestable, since it forced them to show their books and make public the details of their business transactions. To the hangers-on of the party the Catasto was equally unsatisfactory, as affording none of the pecuniary advantages to which they felt themselves entitled as members of the Government.

Therefore by degrees the principle of the Catasto was allowed to fall into desuetude. Not that it was not still used as a basis for a great part of taxation, but it was turned from a safeguard of equality into an instrument of unfairness. This was done in two ways. First, the very principle of the Catasto demanded that it should be regularly re-assessed. Wealth passed rapidly from hand to hand; fortunes were made and lost very quickly; the Catasto, as a tax on property, not on persons, ought to have closely followed the changes in the distribution of wealth. But no re-assessment of the Catasto was made between 1431 and 1458. The work of adjustment was supposed to be done by a small committee, called

"Sgravatori," who were authorised to make additions or deductions according to the supposed increase or decrease in individual incomes. But as these adjustments were made quite arbitrarily by the Sgravatori, and as the Sgravatori were of course members of the ruling party, the result of their estimations may easily be guessed.

Again, in order to obtain favour with the poorer classes, and to prevent complaints from them at the constant imposition of taxes, a new principle was applied to the Catasto in 1443 and again in 1447,—that of the sliding scale, or "Scala," which had first been suggested by the Ciompi. In 1443, by this system, incomes of not more than fifty florins paid 4 per cent at each Catasto; from fifty to a hundred florins paid 7 per cent, and so on, until incomes of fifteen hundred florins and upwards paid $33\frac{1}{2}$ per cent, or a third of the whole. In 1447 the rate was higher and the Scala yet more steeply graduated; incomes under fifty florins paid 8 per cent; over fifteen hundred paid 50 per cent. Of course, in considering these high rates it must not be forgotten that, according to the original plan of the Catasto, many deductions were made from the income before it was rated at all, so that these taxes were not quite so exorbitant as appears at first sight. The entire sums raised certainly seem large. "The war expenditure is seventy thousand florins a month; it is impossible to endure it much longer," was the cry; yet not only was it endured, but Florence was afterwards even more wealthy than before. True, the value of shares in the Monte fell somewhat in Cosimo's life-time, yet after the Peace of Lodi the Government found it possible to decrease the interest paid on them.

The comfort and luxury in which the upper classes lived, and the practical immunity of the poor from taxation indicate sufficiently that Florence could well bear the burden laid upon her. Indeed it is difficult to reconcile what we know of the great extension of commerce, the magnificent buildings, the vast sums spent on public festivals, on dress, art, and private entertainment, with the assertion which has been made that the richer citizens were driven from the town to take refuge in their country houses by the extortions of the tax-gatherers, and that thus the city was impoverished. We have to qualify this statement by confining it to that portion of the rich citizens who were inimical to Cosimo's government.

It must also be remembered that what seems to us one enormous income-tax had at that time, with the assistance of but little indirect taxation, to cover all the expenses of government, both national and municipal, and that these expenses had of late much increased with the rapid development of Florence from a mediæval into a modern state. A greater number of paid troops had to be supported to keep pace with the armies of other states; the extension of territorial possessions necessitated an increase in the expense of defending them; the development of the modern system of diplomacy doubled the number and length of embassies and necessitated expenditure on secret service money. A great deal of this came out of Cosimo's private purse, but not all. And a Florentine versifier aptly described the people who complained of great expenditure as those who "wish Florence to fly, but have plucked out all her feathers."

And it was not the Municeans who suffered from heavy taxation or from the sliding scale. They were able, by the favour of the officials, to have their incomes rated at very much below their real amount, so that only a small portion of it was taxed at all; and beyond this they easily obtained further exemptions or diminutions as they pleased.

It was those who were not favourites of the Government that suffered by taxation, and still more by the forced loans which were constantly demanded from 1442 onwards. Some of these were fixed on the Catasto basis, but in many there was no pretence of adhering to the Catasto. These were arbitrarily assessed by a committee of members of the Government, who could fix an individual quota at any sum they pleased. True, these loans were intended to bear interest, and were sometimes even refunded; but the interest was not regularly paid, and was often forfeited on the pretence that the recipient was behind hand with his taxes.

It was said that Cosimo used the taxes as a weapon "in place of the dagger." Like most Florentines he had scruples against the employment of the latter, but he found the former almost as effective. Men of high character and talents were deliberately ruined in this manner because they showed signs of too much independence. The most famous example was the unfortunate Giannozzo Manetti. For many years he had filled important official positions in the Republic, and had invariably acquitted himself with success. But he was not thought sufficiently devoted to the Medicean interests, and on more than one occasion as ambassador he had failed to adhere to the line of foreign policy which

Cosimo had laid down. It was decided to bring him to submission by heavy taxation. After having paid altogether 135,000 florins, he took refuge with Pope Nicolas V., whose friend he was, but was then summarily ordered home, on pain of exile if he did not obey. So well did he justify himself before the Signory and Colleges, that, in an access of unusual independence, they elected him a member of the next Dieci; but his success in that office caused a fresh attack to be made upon him by means of taxation, and he was at last driven to obtain leave to reside in Rome, where the Pope, who appreciated his great talents, made him one of his secretaries.

And not only was the weapon of taxation employed against enemies and suspected persons; but, "not being able to move by the desire of rewards quiet and unambitious citizens who attended only to their business affairs, they used this weapon to make themselves omnipotent in everything, and to force people to study their wishes in matters of the least importance." A hostile vote in the Councils, a careless speech overheard by an informer, even an effort to maintain a neutral position, all these indications were equally punished.

Just as taxation was used as a system for the reward of supporters and the punishment of opponents of the Medici, so also were the distribution of offices and the administration of justice.

The passion for office-holding was curiously strong in Florence, considering how little substantial power went with the official position. Some offices of course were lucrative, and "there were men in Florence who made their living out of the public offices, so that when one of these was made captain of a town" (one of the subject towns), "it would have been better for that place to have had a whole foreign army quartered upon it." But it was rather the dignity and apparent importance lent by official position which made the citizens "conduct themselves like slaves in their desire to obtain office." A man who "avoided the Palace" and lived quietly, attending to his business, was considered absurdly modest. A regular system of canvassing members of the Accopiatori and Balìa seems to have prevailed. Most powerful was the desire to be a member of the Signory itself,—"In Florence one was hardly looked upon as a man unless one had been at least once a member of the Signory."

Cosimo encouraged this passion by keeping up and increasing the outward dignity of the offices, and particularly of the Signory, while gradually and silently sapping their real power. Appointment to office was the recognised reward for services and devotion to the Government. To be able to appoint his followers to new offices was one of the reasons why Cosimo always longed after the acquisition of Lucca. Many men of older families with hereditary experience in government were excluded, while the officials were "new men," some of them but recently come from the Contado and settled in the city. Yet Guicciardini, the most impartial of judges, asserts that the Medici, who thoroughly understood the business of government, always took care that the offices should be filled by competent persons. The brilliant Matteo Palmieri, of whom Alfonso of Naples said, "If the chemists in Florence are like this, what must the doctors be?" is only one among many examples of men of no family raised to leading positions simply on account of their learning and ability. No one who had once failed the Medici ever had the chance of doing so a second time. Certainly the men whom they appointed to defend the Florentine fortresses were much more faithful and courageous than those selected by the Albizzi government. The fault of the Medici, Guicciardini maintained, lay rather in unjustly excluding many good men from the Government than in ruling by means of unfit or useless men.

Yet, looking upon this aspect of Cosimo's rule in the light of modern politics, it is obvious that to exclude those who were unfavourable to him, however gifted, was a necessity if he meant to maintain his own position in Florence. His predecessors in power had acted in precisely the same manner. Cosimo's position was after all that of the leader of a party, and the exclusion from office of every one even suspected of a hankering after the Albizzi was little more sweeping, if somewhat more violent in its methods, than is in the United States the exclusion of the Radicals from even the pettiest official positions when the Democrats come into power. Cosimo could no more have admitted friends and foes impartially into his government than could our own King William III. succeed in his endeavour to rule as "king of the nation, not of a party."

Less easily justifiable is the administration of justice in favour of the ruling party. Although the fear of offending Cosimo, who had a strong personal aversion to violence unless he thought it absolutely necessary, may have acted as a deterrent against the more violent forms of crime, it was none the less true that a criminal who belonged to, or could obtain the favour of a member of, the ruling party was sure of protection, and, if punished at all, was punished lightly. The charges made by Guicciardini are no doubt founded on fact. The Medici, he declared, recommended their friends to the magistrates, and without their knowledge their adherents did the same, and with great success, because of the fear of their political influence. Members of the ruling party made compacts with powerful persons in the Contado to support one another in crimes and robberies, such as the violent seizure of both private and ecclesiastical property. Those who were oppressed were often silent for fear of offending the powerful robbers. What was a crime in one man was but a venial fault in another: it was almost a proverb that "enemies must be judged with vigour, and friends with leniency." "Rebels and criminals," wrote an Anti-Medicean, "go about secure in Florence under the protection of the Medici, and at their orders criminals are released from the prisons." To those accused of complicity in plots against the Government, justice was unattainable. The evidence of a single informer was accepted against suspected conspirators. The Otto di Balìa, the court composed of the most devoted Mediceans, was that before which they had to appear.

Yet it is very unjust to assert that the blame for this state of affairs lay with the Medici. All over Europe mal-administration of justice prevailed in the Middle Ages. In Florence it was as bad as or worse than anywhere else. The respect for law and legal tribunals had sunk very low; the immense number of lawyers and the intense ignorance and inability of most of them had brought the profession into contempt. There was complete uncertainty as to the actual state of the laws, in the midst of the rapid and radical changes which were constantly made in them. "In Florence," ran a proverb, "a law is made one evening and repealed the next morning"; and Dante complained of this state of things quite as much as Cosimo's contemporaries. The confusion of different kinds of law, ecclesiastical, civil, municipal, the elaboration of forms, the complete liberty left to criminal judges in affixing penalties, all added to the confusion. An old proverb ran, "May sorrow, evil and the lawyers be far from thee!" Corruption was the rule, not the exception; the law was naturally converted into a political weapon, more especially since it carried with it authority for the use of torture.

This state of things was not in the least worse during the Medici rule than before or even after. The accusation of seizing ecclesiastical property had been made against Niccolò Barbadori just as it was made against the Mediceans. Indeed, their settled government tended rather to improve matters, since, though tyrannical themselves, they distinctly preferred law and order to anarchy; even the tyrannous Otto di Balìa was a "real terror to evil-doers." Nor could any judgment under the Medici have been more unfair than that which in 1433 his enemies passed upon Cosimo himself and his relations, in which they were declared guilty of incendiarism, and of conspiracies to ruin, devastate and exterminate Florence, at the very time when Cosimo at least was in retirement in the Mugello.

Yet it may readily be supposed that Cosimo's government was very far from giving satisfaction to a large section of the Florentines. To many of the poor, who had thought that with his rule the Millennium was to begin, there was natural disappointment. "If I had thought," exclaimed the chronicler Cavalcanti, who had been at first Cosimo's ardent admirer, "that the virtues of men could be perpetual, I should have dared to say that Cosimo was a man rather divine than human; but because I knew that prosperity is always followed by ingratitude and pride, I was therefore silent." "The Mediceans," it was complained, "make us worse off than we were before. Once they gave us sweet things, now they give us bitter."

One large class of people, if not enthusiastic followers of the Albizzi, had yet been offended by the violence of the revolution, or had friends and relations who suffered in the following proscriptions. Amongst these was Agnolo Pandolfini, who, on the banishment of Palla Strozzi, retired altogether from public life. Still more were they offended by the political methods of the new Government. They suffered in the law courts from the favour shown there to the Mediceans; they found themselves excluded from the offices and political influence which they considered themselves entitled by hereditary right to enjoy, while their places were taken by men from the Minor Arts, or who had but lately come to settle in the city; "and," says Cavalcanti of the members of the older families thus excluded, "they would all have consented to lose one eye themselves, if he who had brought about this state of things might lose both." The new officials were of course accused of peculation; Puccio Pucci, it was said, had piled up a huge fortune at the expense of the

Commune, for, "since no stream becomes great with pure water only, so no one could become so rich without dishonest gains." He bought up government debts at low rates from the creditors, and then obtained full payment at the public exchequer. The money obtained by taxation, it was asserted, did not all go to the objects for which it was intended; part found its way into the pockets of private citizens. Even Cosimo, although it was known that he voluntarily contributed much towards public expenses, did not escape suspicion, since all the finances of the Republic passed through his hands. His very liberality was condemned; "this," it was said of his building, "is only his hypocrisy and ecclesiastical pride; it is paid for out of our purses under pretence of subsidies for Count Francesco" (Sforza). "Now he has begun to build a palace, which will make the Colosseum of Rome look small. Who indeed would not build magnificently if he could spend other people's money upon it?" One day the doors of the Medici Palace were found to have been smeared with blood, but Cosimo was too wise to take any notice of the insult.

Above all, the heavy taxation was a grievance. Besides the members of the opposition, who really had something to complain of, there was always a large class of professional discontents who would have grumbled quite as noisily at any other government. The violent manner in which the payment of taxes was extorted really was a grievance, though not peculiar to the Medici times; but the irritation caused by taxation was increased tenfold by the unpopularity of the objects to which the taxes were applied. It was hard to have to contribute large sums of money; but harder when they were spent on a foreign policy which was reprobated by all classes, and was only carried through by the force of Cosimo's iron will, against almost universal opposition. The break with the old allies, Venice and the Pope, was disliked only less than the league with the upstart Condottiere on whom such vast sums were lavished. Even the Mediceans disapproved; the Anti-Mediceans, dimly aware that Cosimo was grounding a dynastic power upon his foreign policy, opposed it still more vigorously. Venice found a fair field in Florence for intrigues against the Sforzescan alliance, and against Cosimo himself. Of course when anything went wrong Cosimo had to bear the blame; "I do not say whose fault it was," said the cautious Vespasiano of the failure to obtain a hoped-for peace; "but most people blamed the rulers, and said it was their fault,"—"the rulers" is Vespasiano's euphuism for Cosimo.

The years 1442 and 1443 were those which saw the beginning of Sforza's failures in the March, the Catasto more and more neglected, and the Scala first employed. There was a general feeling of discontent and uneasiness in the city, and this had an opportunity for manifesting itself unpleasantly in the following year. The Accopiatori appointed in 1434 were to hold office only for five years, and the Scrutiny made at the same time was also to be revised at the end of that period. Fresh Accopiatori were appointed and a new Scrutiny made without any difficulty in 1439; but in 1444 the case was altered. It is difficult for us to ascertain what persons were really responsible for making a Scrutiny, probably the Colleges and Councils together; at all events, the spirit of discontent was strong enough to enable the opponents of the Government to pass through the Scrutiny and put into the Borse the names of a number of persons not at all acceptable to the rulers. The Scrutiny was thereupon popularly nicknamed the Scrutiny of the Aliso flower, because it looked beautiful at a distance, but had an unpleasant odour. At the same time there was so much excitement and disturbance generally that Cosimo felt it necessary to act with a firm hand.

His means of recovering his authority was to have a new Balìa appointed, which should make another Scrutiny and elect new Accopiatori. The spirit of independence had not gone very far after all, since the Councils meekly submitted to the appointment of a new Balìa, probably nominated by the Signory at Cosimo's dictation, so that Cosimo was not obliged to have recourse to any violent means, such as a Parliament, in order to obtain it.

The Balìa did what was required of it with regard to the Scrutiny and the Accopiatori,—the Scrutiny of the "Aliso flower" being annulled,—and carried out new proscriptive measures against several persons disliked by the Government. Filippo Pieruzzi, Secretary of the Riformagioni, was dismissed from his office. Perhaps this was a belated piece of revenge, since it was he who had replaced Martino Martini in this very secretaryship in 1429.

Pieruzzi's removal enabled Cosimo, when himself Gonfalonier in the following year, to have a trustworthy committee appointed to draw up new regulations for the management of the Riformagioni, with the purpose, said an unfavourable critic, "of drawing the city more and more under his tyranny."

But the effect of the Balìa of 1444 wore off by degrees, and though in 1448 new Accopiatori were appointed without any disturbance, Cosimo found the difficulty of carrying through his foreign policy continually greater. The opposition came to a head when Florence found herself unwillingly ranged against Venice and suffering from Neapolitan invasions, while Sforza, upon whom so much money had been spent, could give her no assistance, but barely maintain himself at Milan. Some years of scarcity, increased by the depredations of the Neapolitans, brought real distress to the poor, who were not even to be mollified by large distributions of corn at a low price, provided and paid for to a great extent by Cosimo himself. Cosimo had had the greatest difficulty in procuring his own re-election on the Monte in 1446; in 1452, although the term of office of the Accopiatori of 1448 was not yet expired, he found that he could not carry on the war successfully without the support of a new Balìa.

This Balìa, unlike those which preceded it, was to have an indefinite term of office, continuing to supersede the regular Councils until the war should be over. It was not to make a new Scrutiny until 1453, when the term of that of 1448 should be expired, nor was it to elect new Accopiatori; those of 1444 and 1448, in whom it is to be supposed Cosimo felt confidence, were for the future to act together. Amongst other proceedings this Balìa imposed fresh taxes, increased still further the authority of the Otto, who now received supreme power in all criminal cases, whether concerned with the State or not, and again renewed the terms of banishment of the exiles for ten more years.

This sentence fell most cruelly upon the unfortunate Palla Strozzi. Already sixty-six years of age when the revolution of 1434 drove him from his home, Palla had hoped that, by living in blameless retirement and avoiding all communication with the exiles who were plotting against the Government, he might be suffered when the ten years had elapsed to return in peace to Florence. But his submission did not soften his enemies; in 1444 his banishment was renewed with that of the other exiles. Yet Palla hoped against hope that he might live to see Florence once more. One after another his sons were taken from him by death, till he was left almost alone. Yet, after twenty years of exile, the feeble, broken-hearted old man was not allowed to return to die in Florence. Six years after the renewal of his banishment in 1454, Palla died, the saddest, most pathetic victim of that relentless system of perpetual exile which had broken the hearts of so many noble Florentines.

But though complacent in many ways, the Balìa of 1452 did not show itself altogether submissive. In order to enable the Mediceans to command a majority, it was found necessary to alter the usual Florentine law, by which only measures that obtained two-thirds of the votes could be passed, and, instead, to allow one-half to constitute a legal majority. In 1453 the Balìa actually refused to permit Cosimo to dictate to it the names of the persons to be appointed on a new Dieci, until the good news of the promised invasion of Italy by René brought it to a better temper, and it allowed Cosimo to have his way. The fact was that, just as the oligarchy, under the influence of prosperity, had split up into factions, so the Mediceans, secure of their power, were beginning to divide amongst themselves. Had Cosimo been another Rinaldo, it would merely have been a case of the substitution of one oligarchy for another, and the second must have shared the fate of the first. But though Cosimo's individual influence was strong enough to hold his followers together, and to keep all in subordination to himself, it did not preclude a good deal of strife amongst the more ambitious members of the party, and finally an attempt at rebellion against his own authority.

From the first Cosimo, owing his restoration to his adherents, had been unable to rule them absolutely; "his authority," says Guicciardini, "not being firmly grounded, the power of the other members of his party was so great that he had to put up with their infinite extortions." Yet until age descended upon him he was able to keep them well in hand. There is little proof of the rivalry between him and Neri Capponi, which historians have described as coming to a head in 1441. Neri, in spite of Rinaldo's fear of him, was not a man who ever seriously tried to put himself first. He took care, in 1434, to be on the winning side; and his great capabilities and the respect in which he was held made him a valuable ally to the party at that time, and a useful servant afterwards. He was continually in the employment of the Republic—a member of nearly all the Dieci, frequently Commissioner with the troops, often ambassador, usually one of the Accopiatori. In everything which he undertook he was successful; he had a great popularity with the soldiers, and could keep the peace between rival Condottieri, and make them do the work for which they were paid in what seemed to the other harassed Commissioners a truly marvellous manner. There was not a Court or Republic in Italy where he was not held in the highest respect as Ambassador. He seems to have been content with his position; from his own account of his life he appears thoroughly satisfied both with it and with himself; there is no indication that he wished to be considered Cosimo's rival. He did not indeed approve of Cosimo's foreign policy, preferring the Venetian to the Sforzescan alliance; but even Cosimo's most devoted followers were often inclined to agree with him there, and Neri's opposition, though firm, was never extended to any act of overt hostility or rebellion in internal politics.

It is of course possible that Baldaccio d'Anghiari, the Condottiere who was assassinated by order of the Government in 1441, was one of Neri's many military friends, and that Cosimo was afraid of the alliance between them, as Rinaldo degli Albizzi had been of that between Neri and Fortebraccio. Yet the death of Baldaccio is amply accounted for by the use which Cosimo believed the Pope was going to make of him; the theory that Neri was specially interested in the Condottiere rests upon the assertion of only one prejudiced and not very trustworthy contemporary, and it may perhaps be noted that one of the Capponi family was on the Signory at the time, and consented to the assassination. Only a year before this, Neri was labouring gallantly to defend Florence from Piccinino and the exiles, and making special provision for Cosimo's personal safety in case of danger, while very soon afterwards we find him acting on Cosimo's special commission for the reform of the Riformagioni; and, during the very years in which he was opposing Cosimo's foreign policy, he was all the while holding the trusted position of Accopiatore. Just at this time also he was working hand in hand with Cosimo for the restoration of the Bentivogli family in Bologna.

Yet Cosimo no doubt preferred that his able lieutenant should be kept well employed, and for the most part absent from Florence, thus diminishing the danger of any serious rivalry from him. For the rest, Cosimo found him useful to counterbalance the growing power of a younger politician, Luca Pitti, who during the Forties was rapidly coming to the front. He had been one of the Priors who recalled Cosimo, had gained some reputation from his prompt action in the Vitelleschi affair, had acted frequently as Gonfalonier, as an official for the imposition of taxes or on the Dieci, and had been almost permanently one of the Accopiatori. Luca was an "huomo animoso"; "One who would dare much for his friends; excellent as an instrument in other men's hands, but dangerous if allowed to become independent." He was high-spirited, energetic, and daring, as free in speech and bold in action as Cosimo was silent, cautious, and slow; a man who easily gained popularity and quickly made a party, but was incapable of steady persistence in any line of policy, and, if easily leading others, was equally amenable to others' influence.

The older generation of politicians seems by this time to have passed away; we hear no more of Alamanno Salviati or of Puccio Pucci. Averardo de'

Medici died at Venice without ever returning from exile,—a fortunate circumstance perhaps for Cosimo, since Averardo's unpopularity was as great as his own popularity, and Averardo's powers of doing mischief would have been practically unlimited. His part as the devoted cousin was taken by a younger man, Bernadetto de' Medici, who was throughout Cosimo's most faithful and trusted friend, and was admitted with Cosimo's own sons into those family councils by which the city was practically ruled. Lorenzo de' Medici died in 1440; he was his brother's faithful follower, but had little of his ability,—"Cosimo the fox, Averardo the wolf, Lorenzo the cow," spitefully said Filelfo the Humanist.

But besides Luca Pitti there were two other politicians, somewhat Cosimo's juniors, who from 1447 onwards played leading parts. One of these was Dietisalvi Neroni, whose father Nerone had been instrumental in recalling Cosimo from exile. Dietisalvi was a clever and able man, much trusted by Cosimo, and admitted by him more nearly into the secrets of his policy than any one else out of his family. He acted as Accopiatore during the greater part of Cosimo's rule, and was no doubt one of Cosimo's specially trusted agents on that committee. He alone loyally supported Cosimo's foreign policy with regard to Sforza, and during the critical year 1453, as a member of the Dieci, he pressed Cosimo's views upon that unwilling body.

Not less important was Agnolo Acciaiuoli, who had suffered exile with Cosimo and with him returned in triumph. Since that time he had acted loyally under him, had been employed as Accopiatore and on many foreign embassies. He seems at first to have been unwilling to embrace the new foreign policy, but after Sforza's conquest of Milan was quite converted to the advantage of his alliance. It was through Acciaiuoli's skilful negotiations that the league with France was concluded, and René brought to Italy. He was therefore "one of the principal citizens, and could do what he wished in the city."

During the years which preceded 1454, these more ambitious spirits were kept employed in foreign politics, and had little time to think about their position at home. But the Peace of Lodi, by putting an end to their occupations, gave them leisure to turn their thoughts to internal politics, and to discover that, while Cosimo was growing old, and his son Piero showed no special signs of political talent, they were in the full flower of their age, and had just been proving their capabilities in organisation and diplomacy. It was natural that they should think it possible to change the character of the government by acquiring a greater share in the supreme power themselves, to revert in fact from the rule of one to the rule of several. They must have felt it impossible to do without Cosimo altogether, since it was upon his wealth and foreign connections that the supremacy of the party was based. The place of *primus inter pares* might be conceded to him, but to Cosimo, intent upon founding a family dominion, such a position was not likely to give satisfaction.

It seemed to Pitti, Neroni and Acciaiuoli, the leaders of a new opposition, that Cosimo's authority was chiefly maintained by the Balìa; therefore their first measure was to take advantage of the excuse furnished by the conclusion of peace to put an end to its authority. This was done in June 1454, when Neroni was Gonfalonier, and so popular was the measure that only twenty-six in the Council of the People, and seven in that of the Commune opposed it. The removal of the Balìa had little result, however, as long as the Scrutiny which it had made was still in force, and the Accopiatori whom it had appointed still exercised their office. In November of the same year, therefore, when Agnolo Acciaiuoli was Gonfalonier, a new Scrutiny was made to supersede that drawn up by the Balìa, and immediately afterwards, during the first Signory of 1455, a still further step was taken, and it was ruled that, from the July following, the power of the Accopiatori was to cease, and the Signory once more be chosen by lot.

What precisely Pitti and his party hoped to gain by these measures it is very difficult to ascertain from the vague accounts which have reached us. They were all Accopiatori themselves, Pitti, Neroni, Acciaiuoli and Agnolo della Stufa, who was Gonfalonier in January 1455, and they must have arranged their own elections as Gonfaloniers in order to carry out these measures. But in putting an end to the office of Accopiatori, they appear to have been deliberately cutting away their own power. On the other hand, they do not seem always to have commanded a majority of the Accopiatori, and perhaps they hoped that the chances of the lot might be more favourable to them. When Acciaiuoli was made Gonfalonier in November 1454, Neri Capponi had succeeded, in spite of their opposition, in forcing into the Signory a youth of great capability and courage, Pandolfo Pandolfini, grandson of the famous Agnolo.

Pandolfo successfully withstood many of the measures which Acciaiuoli wished to have passed, amongst them one for rendering the Priors powerless to act without the Gonfalonier,— an arrangement which would have made the control of the Signory easier to the Government, since it would then have been necessary to manage only one man instead of nine. Acciaiuoli also intended to make new proscriptions; he said that he wanted to settle affairs in Florence, "so that there could be no more disturbances about them." "Every one in Florence trembled," each thinking his turn was come, "and there was so much terror in the city that it seemed as if not only the citizens trembled but the walls also." Pandolfo contrived, however, to frustrate all Acciaiuoli's plans, and in particular to save one citizen of great importance, perhaps Neri himself, whom the Gonfalonier wished to banish.

So far Cosimo had made no attempt to interfere openly. Neri had been there to check the independence of the Accopiatori if it went too far, and Pandolfini was rewarded not long afterwards by an appointment as official of the Monte. Cosimo was quite clever enough to see that in abolishing the office of Accopiatori the new party were cutting their own throats. His personal reputation and influence secured his own position; and he felt that, when the right opportunity came, he would easily be able to recover anything he might temporarily lose. The numbers of the new party were not sufficient and its individual members not influential enough to be able to establish a powerful oligarchy, nor was Cosimo's personal popularity amongst the lower classes extended to them. They had no influence independent of him; their real importance was merely as members of the Medicean party. So Cosimo quietly waited, and let them feel the result of their own hot-headedness.

The revival of appointment by lot was of course a very popular measure. It was accepted in the Councils by large majorities. The first result was, as might have been expected, an end to the monopoly of office which Pitti and his friends had hitherto enjoyed. The next, which they had by no means contemplated, was a re-assessment of the Catasto, the work of a very independent Signory at the beginning of 1458. A few months before, one of the opportunities for acquiring ill-gotten wealth had been removed by a law which made it illegal to buy up public debts at a low rate, and then obtain full payment of them from the Commune. This touched the pockets of a good many hangers-on of the Medici party; but they felt the restoration of the Catasto to be much worse. An entirely new register of property, after the method of the original Catasto, would of course include all the gains they had made since 1431, and most of them had in those twenty-seven years prospered exceedingly. Above all, they dreaded the application of the Scala to all this newly-acquired wealth. All the pecuniary advantages which they had possessed as members of the governing party were gone in an instant if taxation was no longer to be arbitrarily assessed by themselves in their own favour, but was to be imposed on a regular system in proportion to the means of the payers.

Cosimo, with his vast wealth, cared little personally whether he were taxed by Catasto or not. What paid under any system of taxation was a trifle to the sums which he privately devoted to the service of the State. Yet Cosimo hesitated whether to approve or not. Nicodemo wrote to Sforza, "On the one hand, he does not want to offend the rich, on the other he does not wish to lose the favour of the common people, who all wish for the Catasto. . . . If the Catasto does not pass the Council of the People," he added, "the city will be all upside down; perhaps there will be a revolution. Bernadetto de' Medici and Dietisalvi Neroni are both much disturbed about it." The Catasto did, however, pass all the Councils, and then Pitti and his party were left to consider how to improve the situation into which they had brought themselves. The remedy which immediately occurred to them was a new Balìa, a new Scrutiny, new Accopiatori, the resumation, in fact, of the reins of government into the hands of the party. But they were powerless to carry through a measure requiring so much skill and so great authority without Cosimo's help, and Cosimo, willing that they should learn how ill they could do without him, positively refused, when approached on the subject, to sanction the renewal of the Balìa, unless it could be obtained in the ordinary way through the Colleges and Councils, and would not listen to the suggestion of holding a Parliament. But the Councils, having found their power, were not willing to surrender it. Even the Signory, far from supporting the Gonfalonier of March 1458 in his proposal for a new Balìa, made a law by which Balìa could only be obtained from the Signory, Colleges, and Councils by unanimous votes in all of these bodies.

But Luca Pitti was the next Gonfalonier but one,

and he was determined to succeed by fair means or foul. He first proposed to the Councils to appoint a new Balìa, which they indignantly refused to do. Unluckily for himself, Girolamo Machiavelli, a somewhat hot-headed but well-intentioned person, with Republican ideas, made a speech in one of the Councils declaiming against Balìas generally, and all other attempts to destroy the freedom of the citizens. Not a moment was lost in arresting Machiavelli on the charge of calling the Signory tyrants; "he had disseminated new terms of tyrant and slave in a free city." Where a plot is wanted, a plot is usually found. Machiavelli was in correspondence with other citizens who shared his Republican views. There were arrests, examinations by torture, confessions, all the paraphernalia of a full-blown conspiracy. Nothing but a Balìa could act vigorously enough in so dangerous a crisis, Pitti maintained; and Cosimo, deprived of the services of Capponi by his death, thought that the experiment in "free government" had lasted long enough, that the too independent members of his party must have learned their lesson, and that it was time to tighten again the reins of power. He thought it best, in order to impress the ignorant at home, and any foreign governments which might have fancied his power to be waning, to make a demonstration of his strength by holding a parliament. How this design succeeded we learn from the letters to Sforza of Nicodemo, and of the Podestà, also a Milanese, upon this occasion. Their accounts are worth quoting. "To-morrow," wrote Nicodemo, a few days before the Parliament, "the lord of Faenza" (a Condottiere in the service of Florence) "will arrive here with 300 horse and 50 foot, besides the troops of Simonetto. On Thursday troops of country people will arrive. The morning of the day fixed for the Parliament, they will range themselves in order of battle upon the piazza. All the citizens will be there without arms. The Signory will read a list of a number of citizens to whom Balìa shall be given for the reform of the town, and will then ask the people if they are satisfied. The well-disposed will cry 'Yes! Yes!' and the people, according to custom, will all do the same. The Signory, exultant, will retire from the Ringhiera into the Palace, and the fête will be over. Then, little by little, the number of members of the Balìa will be decreased; only a few will remain, who will reform the State according to their wishes." . . . "Piero di Cosimo" (Cosimo's son) "arrived in Florence to-day. He wishes to be present at the performance, which rarely takes place, but will be unattended by danger. . . . Cosimo acts very cautiously, and likes to appear neutral." In spite of the harmlessness of the "performance," great precautions were taken that it should go off without a hitch. Numerous secret meetings were held by members of the party to arrange the details. In Cosimo's house was a great collections of arms "worth a treasure; nowhere else in Italy could such a great number be found." Piero's wife and children were left in safety at the country house. But all passed off well. "This morning," wrote Nicodemo, "between ten and eleven o'clock the Parliament was held with the greatest possible unanimity and without the least disturbance. . . . They made a Balìa as they wished, by which they can settle the taxes and elections and all the government according to their desires." The Podestà wrote, "As the names of the Balìa were read out, they were unanimously accepted by all the people without the least uproar. It appeared to me most astonishing. If I had not been present I could not have believed that such a great crowd of people could be assembled, after the late agitations, without any disturbances arising. All called with one voice 'Si! Si! Fiat! Fiat!'"

The first work of the new Balìa was to follow up the conspiracy which Pitti believed himself to have unearthed, but Cosimo took care that the prosecutions should not go far, and that the supposed conspirators should escape with their lives. Nicodemo at least understood that their punishment was merely intended as a warning to other ambitious Republicans. "They have beaten the kittens in order to frighten the lions," he wrote home, "and to show them that if they will not be tamed their turn will come next. But they too shiver, and promise to behave like good children." The Balìa did its duty about Scrutiny, Accopiatori, and new taxes; its last and most important act was the creation of a body intended to enable the Government to dispense altogether with Balìas for the future. The necessity of frequently renewing them had caused constant fresh irritation; it was a reminder of the partial suspension of the Constitution very unpleasant to a people that at least liked to call itself free. Yet it was evidently necessary for the Government to have a body, more regular and more trustworthy than the Colleges and Councils, to elect Accopiatori and to make Scrutinies. For this purpose therefore the Balìa created in 1459 a new council, called the Council of a Hundred. It was to consist only of those who had duly passed the Scrutinies and had been members of a Signory since 1434, so that it could be depended upon to appoint government nominees as Accopiatori. It had indeed the same powers as the other Councils, and was to be consulted "on all matters of State," but its main function was to act as an elective body for the Accopiatori. We may consider it as Cosimo's latest endeavour towards solving the problem of how to keep the official executive well within his own control.

Luca Pitti was able, during the period of his office as Gonfalonier, to temper the bitterness of the newly restored Catasto for himself and his fellow merchants. It was clear from the returns of the lately appointed assessors that many business-men did not show them their real books, but purposely falsified copies. It was therefore arranged that they should be allowed to make compositions with the assessors for that part of the tax which was to be levied on their business profits. No doubt Pitti and his friends were able to make compositions highly favourable to themselves.

For the last six years of Cosimo's life the Government ran to all appearance smoothly enough. Cosimo recovered in the main his old authority, but the weight of years and ill-health pressed heavily upon him,—"he cannot be always in the Palace as he used to be,"—and to secure peace at home, in order that he might have a free hand in carrying out his foreign policy, he was obliged to leave a good deal of the show of power to Luca Pitti. Pitti began to be looked upon as the rising, Cosimo as the sinking, star in politics. People who wanted favour with the magistrates paid court to the younger man, followed him about, and made him presents as if he were a prince. Pitti, carried away by his sudden popularity, bore himself in princely fashion; he began to build two magnificent palaces, one five miles from Florence, the other on the rising ground just beyond the south bank of the Arno, which was intended to outshine far the modest family mansion of the Medici in the Via Larga. His party, which included Acciaiuoli and Neroni, was accordingly nicknamed the "Mountain"; the Mediceans who remained faithful to Cosimo were called the "Plain," because the Via Larga was in the level part of the town. To this day the huge pile of building which Luca Pitti began, and which after his fall was completed by his rivals, whose property it became, frowns across the valley, a monument of the hopeless vanity of the man who tried to out-do the Medici in their own arts.

But at the moment all smiled on Pitti. It was understood that people who wanted advancement could not do better than assist in his house-building, so that he got much of his labour and materials free. Just before Cosimo's death, he had himself knighted by the Commune in great state, the ceremony being performed by three knights appointed for the purpose. There was a great feast and procession; Pitti seemed for the moment the most prominent person in the city. But Cosimo, who had never seen the necessity of knighthood for himself, and had always preferred to remain a plain citizen, was able to gauge correctly Pitti's character and ambitions. "You aspire after the infinite, I seek only the finite," he said to Pitti in a moment of unusual expansiveness; "you would climb up to the heavens, I wish to mount but little above the earth, and I do not try to fly, for fear of falling. . . . You and I are like two big dogs, who, coming together, sniff at one another; then, because each knows the other to have teeth, they separate and go about their business; will you then attend to your own business, and I will attend to mine!" Pitti was obliged to act on the advice so long as the adviser lived; but the disappointment of his failure in 1454-58 smouldered on to burst into a flame so soon as Cosimo's strong hand was removed.

Acciaiuoli also considered himself to have his grievances. Giannozzo Manetti, whom Cosimo had treated with such severity, was his intimate friend. Cosimo too had disappointed him of the Archbishopric of Pisa, which he wanted for his son, while Cosimo secured it for his own cousin, Filippo de' Medici. Of Dietisalvi Neroni the Milanese envoy wrote in 1463, "Cosimo and his people have no greater nor more ambitious enemy than he."

Cosimo was quite conscious of this opposition, and it troubled him not a little. Pitti might be a dreamer; but at least he was a "big dog," too formidable to be attacked and beaten like a Giannozzo Manetti. Cosimo complained to Nicodemo about him that "one of the greatest, or perhaps the greatest temptation which he had in this world consisted in this, that our Lord God allowed such vicious and deceitful men to live so long."

As he knew his own death to be approaching, Cosimo felt more and more that he left his descendants but ill-fitted to withstand the attacks of such determined adversaries. His favourite and most capable son, Giovanni, was already dead. Piero was in constant ill-health, and inherited his father's slowness in action, without, apparently, his forethought and tenacity. Piero's sons were as yet children. It must have seemed to the old man as if the dynastic power that he had spent so many years and so much labour upon building up would vanish like a shadow after his death. He said to a friend that, "knowing the character of my fellow-citizens, I am sure that in fifty years' time nothing will remain of my rule except the buildings which I have accomplished; and I know that at my death my sons will be involved in more trouble than the sons of any citizen of Florence who has died for many years." Cosimo prophesied correctly for the immediate, but not for the distant, future.

CHAPTER VI

CHARACTER AND BASES OF COSIMO'S RULE—
HIS PRIVATE LIFE

THE foundation of the Medici power in Florence is altogether the most remarkable among the many remarkable political phenomena of the fifteenth century in Italy. The Medici rule was of a character quite distinct from the numerous other tyrannies established in Italian states both before and after this date. It was founded upon a partially popular movement, and was chiefly maintained by popular support; it was government by opinion, not by force. Cosimo had no official position which could enable him to apply effective coercion in any branch of the administration. His place on the Monte did indeed give him control of the expenditure of the Republic, but the controller of expenditure has little power unless he can be certain of obtaining money to spend. And beyond this Cosimo had no official authority. Throughout the thirty years of his government, he was but six months Gonfalonier; though frequently, he was not invariably a member of the numerous Dieci appointed. Once only he went on a foreign embassy, to Venice in 1438. Except on this occasion, he adhered to the rule laid down by Gino Capponi for his son, but which was neglected fatally both by Neri himself and by Rinaldo degli Albizzi,— "He who wishes for a great position in his native city should not leave it too often." A few soldiers, collected by the Signory which recalled Cosimo to guard the Palace and keep order in the town, were dismissed by Cosimo himself as soon as he was Gonfalonier. There were very few people in Florence to whom, and very few matters on which, he could give any direct commands. It is impossible to call a government, which rested so completely on the open acquiescence of the governed, an ordinary tyranny.

Yet, throughout his life, not excepting the years in which Luca Pitti exercised a show of power, Cosimo was practically absolute in all matters about which he chose to exert his authority. Pope Pius II., a political observer of no mean power, gave as his opinion that "nothing is denied to Cosimo; he is judge of war and peace, moderator of the laws; not so much a citizen as lord of the country; the policy of the Republic is settled in his house; he gives commands to the magistrates. Nothing regal is wanting to him but the name and state of a king."

Sforza's envoy, who had opportunities for judging on the spot, told his master, "When you want anything particularly, write in private to Cosimo of your desire, and you will be certain to obtain it." . . . "It is Cosimo who does everything." . . . "Without him nothing is done."

What qualities were there in Cosimo, and what combination of circumstances was there in the Florence of his time, that enabled him to obtain this power over her? The Florentines were not a stupid and passive people, easily enslaved; they had no military ambitions which needed a dictator for their execution; there had been no great internal convulsion which needed an absolute ruler for its pacification. On the contrary, no people in ancient or modern history have been more keenly intellectual, more alive to every aspect of life and eager for all its experiences, more interested in politics, and more anxious to have a share in their own government. It was no small feat for a private citizen, depending merely upon his own brains and his wealth, to establish so wide an authority in such a city-state; and not only to establish and maintain it, but to leave it so firmly grounded that his son, with little of his political ability, was able to hand it on intact to the third generation.

Perhaps the first secret of his power lies in its limitations. Cosimo never attempted the impossible; he was content with what he had obtained, and strove after nothing that was not absolutely essential. To control the appointment of the chief officials, to direct the foreign policy, and, indirectly, to manage the taxation of the Republic, was the extent of his ambitions,—not a small one, indeed, but yet not unlimited. Except in a few cases he showed much respect for the forms of liberty to which Florence was attached; since "in Florence, 'Liberty' was not less engraven on the hearts of men than on her walls and banners." "The equality of the citizens," that is, the theoretical political equality of which they boasted, was preserved—in theory; and, no doubt, as in modern England the absolutism of the democracy is modified by ancient monarchic and aristocratic forms, so in Florence the democratic forms of the official government really modified the despotism of the ruler.

The outward dignity of the offices was maintained, even increased. The palace of the Signory was restored and enlarged, and much money was spent on furniture, ornaments, and plate for their use. The Gonfalonier took the place hitherto occupied by the Podestà at the head of processions; he received the banner which was the emblem of office from the hands of the outgoing Gonfalonier, instead of from the Podestà. The priors, by a curious sophism, were henceforth to be called the "Priors of Liberty," instead of the "Priors of the Arts." Not only the apparent dignity, but also certain very real powers of the Colleges and Councils were preserved. The large minorities, sometimes even majorities, against government measures show that the Councils were not entirely dependent. Cosimo had often serious difficulty in getting money; his re-election on the Monte in 1447 was obtained only with a great effort; even the Balìa was not always amenable, as when in 1453 it made difficulties about accepting Cosimo's selection of candidates for the Dieci.

Still more real was the individual opposition which Cosimo met, sometimes even from his most intimate friends and devoted supporters. "Their method of consultation on affairs of state with the leading citizens," wrote Guicciardini, "and of executing them by means of magistrates, was a great bridle on any violent measures which the Medici might have wished to employ; it did not prevent them from doing anything that they had made up their minds to do, but it often directed their actions into the right channel; . . . they did not think themselves able to act without the counsel of their friends, and they always remained of the opinion that it was best to act so as to satisfy the people, yet rather in internal than in foreign affairs." And it must always be remembered that Cosimo had to manage personally ten or twenty Accopiatori or ten members of the Dieci before he could get Signories appointed, or military and diplomatic business conducted according to his wishes.

All this may seem to be rather a diminution than an increase of Cosimo's power; yet, since it was precisely all this which made the Florentines acquiesce in his rule, —and on the whole acquiesce cheerfully,—it was rather a secret of his strength than a mark of his weakness. Guicciardini knew this also. If the Medici had tried to seize absolute power by force, he maintained, they could have done so, but it would have greatly increased the discontent and disaffection within the city. It would have taken all the life out of the Republic, and weakened it so much that the position of ruler would no longer have been worth having; "for if the Medici had seized absolute lordship, they would have diminished, not increased, their reputation." But they knew, he continued, that "all their affairs depended on the power and reputation of the Republic; in its exaltation and prosperity lay their exaltation and prosperity, because when it was greatest then were they most powerful."

Again, it was this very intangibility of his power, its want of official position, its absence of direct responsibility, which made attack upon it so difficult. Cosimo's one office on the Monte was vigorously attacked; but beyond that there was nothing definite in his authority which could be seized upon by his enemies and used as a handle against him. For example, Luca Pitti's attempt to diminish Cosimo's power by the abolition of the Balìa and the introduction of appointment by lot did not succeed in reaching its real source; neither his personal influence nor his wealth were touched; and Luca's weapons merely rebounded upon their maker.

And, when Cosimo chose, he could easily control all elements of independence. When he wished a certain Donato Acciaiuoli to be made capable of becoming Gonfalonier, he had but to mention his desire to one of the Accopiatori, who at the next meeting of the committee said, "Cosimo wishes Donato Acciaiuoli to be put into the Borse of the Gonfaloniers," and it was immediately done. He could keep the Dieci in order, and instil a proper respect into them by refusing one day to give them an interview, on the pretext that "he had taken medicine." He could tame Luca Pitti by refusing to allow him to hold a Parliament, and yet have the Parliament held, and without any disturbances, when he judged it necessary for securing the authority of the party.

It is clear therefore that it was Cosimo's own great ability which enabled him, more than anything else, to take and keep the position he held. The opportunity was offered: he knew how to seize and how to use it, when to advance and when to retreat, when to conceal his power and when to make an exhibition of it. The moderation which he could show when he chose was not the least mark of his talents. Absolutely unscrupulous,—"States are not to be preserved by paternosters" is one of the cynical sayings attributed to him, —utterly callous to suffering when he judged it necessary to secure his own position, he yet exhibited both scruples and clemency when anything could be gained by them. He never made an unnecessary enemy, nor wished to have an unnecessary punishment inflicted. "He never spoke ill of any one himself, and it displeased him to hear others spoken ill of in his presence." Whenever it was possible he avoided violence, above all he disliked bloodshed; his means of dealing with Baldaccio d'Anghiari was an exception to, not an example of, his methods. In this he was in sympathy with the Florentines, who were fastidious about bloodshed to an extent very unusual in fifteenth-century Italy. Commines, who knew Cosimo only by reputation, had heard that "his authority was soft and amiable, and such as is necessary for a free town."

And Cosimo was moderate in the assumption of the appearance of power. Possessing no official position, he never assumed the state attendant upon office. While the Gonfalonier to whom Cosimo dictated marched in state at the head of his procession, and was everywhere treated with the utmost deference, Cosimo never claimed any state or outward deference, and had to be elected Gonfalonier when he desired to take the leading part in welcoming the Pope to the Council of Florence. He respected too that passion for the appearance of social equality which was part of the Florentine nature. "He dressed like a peasant, and lived like a king," said a contemporary, not very accurately, for Cosimo had a great opinion of the effect of the respectable well-to-do citizen's red gown,—"Dress in red, and don't talk," was his advice to an empty-headed person who wished to appear important,—while life in the houses of the Medici was of the simplest, except when important visitors had to be entertained. Cosimo never fell into Pitti's mistake, never behaved like a prince, nor built a princely dwelling-house. "Envy is a plant which should not be watered," he said. His manners, on the contrary, were always those of the citizen; his house only that of the wealthy merchant. For the latter he rejected Brunelleschi's magnificent design, and chose the more modest plans of Michelozzo. And Cosimo took care not to outrage the Florentine love of social equality by attempting to obtain foreign marriages for his family, as a prince would have done with a view to alliances; but his sons and daughters-in-law were chosen from citizen families whom he favoured. It was said that the reason of the Count of Poppi's rebellion was that Cosimo had refused to marry one of his sons to the Count's daughter.

The avoidance of the appearance of power helped Cosimo also to escape some of its responsibility. When anything disagreeable was to be done, he always found some one to do it for him, taking care never to soil his own fingers. It was his followers who got the blame for the proscriptions of 1434-35, Luca Pitti for the Parliament of 1458, the reigning Gonfalonier for the murder of Baldaccio d'Anghiari. It was only in matters of foreign policy that Cosimo was fully credited with his own acts, and in foreign policy he really wished to seem, as well as to be, responsible, in order that the ultimate success which he anticipated might redound only to his own credit, and in order that the foreign Powers might clearly understand that it was he alone with whom they had to deal. So cleverly was Cosimo's absolutism disguised that simple folk still fancied him only " the first citizen," and never guessed how nearly he was a despot. One Florentine contemporary writer is content to enumerate him among the famous men of his time as " Cosimo di Giovanni de' Medici, who was called in all the world 'the great merchant'; " and he goes on to tell how people said to any one particularly conceited, " Oh you think you are Cosimo de' Medici!"—a recognition of great importance certainly, but not of political supremacy.

But the innermost secret of Cosimo's power lay in his skill in managing both classes and individuals. His power over individuals has been mentioned already in describing his methods with the members of the official government, and especially with those numerous lesser officers, chosen by himself from among all classes, elevated to importance by him, attached to his interests, dependent on him for advancement, rewarded for good service by higher offices, punished for any attempt at independence by exclusion from the Government and heavy taxation.

Amongst classes, those which he took most trouble to conciliate were the Minor Arts and the labouring poor, who belonged to no Art at all. These he conciliated by the opportunities offered to their cleverer members of attaining political position, by sparing them as much as possible the burdens of taxation, by providing them with food in times of scarcity at his own expense or that of the State, by his profuse liberality in almsgiving, by providing regular and well-paid employment on his buildings, and by his generosity to the Church, to which the poorer classes were still strongly attached. Another popular measure of his later years was the building of model dwelling-houses for the poor at State expense, to compensate them for the crowding from which they had suffered, consequent upon the great building activity of the rich at this time.

It should be noted, however, that though Cosimo's power actually rested upon a popular basis, he did not admit the poor as a class to any greater share in the government than that which they had previously enjoyed, but only certain of their individual members whom he raised from the lower to the upper classes. He kept his popularity with the poor by the economic advantages which they enjoyed under his rule, while he continued to govern by means of the upper classes, thus keeping both sections of the community contented, and at the same time blurring the distinctions between them.

It was for the entertainment of the poor particularly that the great public festivals were organised,—the grand funerals of eminent men, the receptions of distinguished visitors, and the tournaments, processions, balls, and beast-shows held in their honour. In all of these the people could take part as spectators without paying anything for seeing the sights. There was nothing a mediæval Italian enjoyed so much as a fine spectacle; and, since there was no court in Florence, Cosimo gladly seized any opportunity that offered itself for gratifying the public taste. At the same time these public shows often served another useful end, to impress her visitors with the wealth and magnificence of Florence. When young Galeazzo Sforza and Pope Pius II. met in Florence in 1459, an eight days' fête of more than usual grandeur was held. On the evening of Pius's arrival a tournament was held in the Piazza S^a Croce by the light of torches. A few days later there was one of the popular open-air balls in the Mercato Nuovo, in which only the noblest youth and beauty in Florence might perform; but every dweller in the city, however humble, was permitted to look on. Next came a chase of wild beasts in the piazza of the Signoria, the people watching from their roofs and windows; but this was rather a failure on account of the unnecessarily "angelic" behaviour of the lions. The same evening a magnificent "Trionfo" (triumphal procession) wound its way through the streets. First walked twenty young gentlemen, and a company of men on foot carrying wands of varying colours. Four gaily-decked horses drew a golden chariot, surmounted by a golden tower. Round about it lads carrying lanterns on long wands seemed to form a veritable garland of fire. On the tower was a young man intended to personate Love. He was arrayed in flesh-coloured tights, with brightly-coloured wings. His eyes were blindfolded, and he carried a bow and arrows. Behind came a banner and some trumpets. Amongst the many youths of great families who took part in this procession were Lorenzo de' Medici, Cosimo's eldest grandson, two young Pazzi, a Pucci, and a son of Dietisalvi Neroni. And this festival was only a rather brilliant example amongst many.

Cosimo's wealth was useful to him not only in enabling him to please the poor, but also in conciliating the richer merchant class. To Florence, after long years of struggle and battle, at first for existence, then for increase of dominion, peace and the opportunity to develop her trade seemed the most desirable of objects. The old military ambitions were dead long since with the military spirit. The upper trading classes thought of little but making their fortunes by commerce, for Florence was quite literally "a city of shopkeepers." It was because Cosimo gave them the opportunity to do this that the Florentines allowed him to absorb their political powers, and reduce them to the level of his subjects.

So long as political strife was waging furiously within the city, it was not possible for the leading merchants to co-operate peacefully for the extension of their business without. But the rule of a master put an end to the passionate faction fighting; the rich families drew together, and formed trading companies with one another, of which the largest and most prosperous was that which bore the Medici name, but included half a dozen families besides the Medici themselves. Cosimo was continually expanding his own business; at one time we find him holding the castle of Assisi as a pledge from Eugenius IV.; afterwards, as banker to Nicolas V., he largely extended his influence in the Papal Court. When Florence was at war with Naples, Cosimo could seriously hamper Alfonso by withdrawing credit from him. The Medici extended their financial transactions yet further by means of their branch houses in Paris, Bruges and London. We find one of their agents furnishing Edward IV. of England with 20,000 crowns to assist him in recovering his kingdom; the loan was not financially profitable, but it widened the Medici connections, and soon afterwards another of their agents acted as security between Edward IV. and Duke Charles of Burgundy for 50,000 crowns.

Where the Medici led the other trading-houses could follow; the close alliance with France stimulated commercial relations with that country, while those of Venice suffered proportionately. The long struggle against Venice which Cosimo undertook was merely the outcome of the commercial strife waged between the two cities, which, at first only rivals for the leadership of Italian trade, became at last rivals for the mastery in the whole sphere of Italian politics.

"A town to sell, if it can find a purchaser," was once said bitterly of Florence, and Cosimo did almost literally purchase it. Not only did he deliberately buy adherents, paying their taxes, bribing them by lucrative offices, dowering their daughters,—he used to say that "his greatest error was in not having begun to spend money earlier than he did,"—but the commercial advantages which he could offer to those who gave him their political support showed the merchants where their interests lay, while resistance to his authority was punished by commercial as well as political ruin.

But Cosimo did not only reach the Florentines through their purses; he had the good fortune to be intimately in sympathy with them in many ways. Besides being the first merchant in a city of merchants, he was the first patron of the new art and the new learning in which the Florentines were so passionately interested. He was able to flatter their craving for a dignified position in international affairs. Florence, the mediator between the Italian states, the ally of the greatest king in Europe, setting up a Duke of Milan at her will, checking the ambition of Venice, magnificently entertaining emperors, popes, and all manner of potentates,—it was worth while to be a Florentine to share in all this. Not the least brilliant of Cosimo's achievements was the removal of the Council held by Pope Eugenius IV. from Ferrara to Florence. Cosimo spared no pains, risking even an open quarrel with Venice to secure this. The Greek potentates were entertained with truly regal hospitality; and, when the solemn Te Deum of thanksgiving for the union of the Eastern with the Western Church was sung in their cathedral, the Florentines must indeed have felt that their money and trouble were not wasted. Nor was the visit of the Emperor without substantial fruits in privileges for the Florentine merchants trading in Constantinople. In the same way, Cosimo arranged that the great general meeting of the Franciscan Order held in 1449 should take place in Florence, the Republic contributing a thousand florins towards its expenses.

Another method of which Cosimo made much use amongst the richer Florentines was that of forming and working through family alliances. The family bond was still of great importance in a state just emerging from mediævalism; the family was not always united,— there are several instances like that of Luca degli Albizzi, Rinaldo's brother, who was an ardent Medicean; but it was at least always supposed to hold together, and the members were considered to be to a great extent responsible for each other. When one member of a family had held an office, the rest were excluded from it,—

"divieti" it was called,—for a fixed period. Whole families, the innocent members as well as the guilty, suffered in the proscriptions of 1434 and 1458. Marriage alliances were considered of the utmost importance; it was one of the recognised rewards conferred by the Medici to arrange a marriage between a member of their own house, or of a house already connected with them, and one of the family to be favoured. Young Piero de' Pazzi, belonging to a wealthy family, whose members, as old allies of Uzzano, were "without the State,"—without the pale of the governing party,—and much oppressed by taxation, had the good fortune to form a friendship with Piero de' Medici; this led to the marriage of another of the Pazzi with Bianca de' Medici, Piero's daughter; and accordingly soon afterwards the Pazzi "obtained the State," and were relieved from excessive taxation. Cosimo was extremely careful about the marriages contracted between members of all families that were of any importance, and frequently interposed to help on or hinder matches of which he approved or disapproved, particularly taking care to prevent matrimonial alliances between two families already suspected of disaffection. How far this interference extended we learn from an entry in the private diary of a citizen of no very great importance, Luca da Panzano by name: "To-day Giovanni di Cosimo de' Medici sent for me, Luca, and said, 'I wish to give as wife to your son Antonio the daughter of Niccolò Fabrini . . . he is . . . a good merchant and good citizen and a friend of the present government.' I answered that what he wished I looked upon as a command, and that I was content."

Cosimo was able to rely not a little upon his influence

in the Contado, and with the subject towns. How his popularity on the rural districts was originally obtained we have no means of discovering. In the Mugello, where he had large estates, on which no doubt he showered his customary liberalities, the affection with which he was regarded is not surprising. Here the peasants and small towns vigorously resisted Piccinino's invasion in 1440,—"not a house was surrendered to the invaders for love of Rinaldo"; but the resistance of the Casentino on the same occasion was no less obstinate. When Cosimo was imprisoned in 1433, men from the Romagnol Alps and other country districts hastened to offer aid to his relations; when he left Florence an exile, the peasants of the Pistojan "Mountain" flocked to meet him and do him honour. Yet Cosimo was not a man apparently calculated by nature to win the hearts of the poor and ignorant; he had no popular gifts like Luca Pitti; he was silent, reserved, cynical. But he was certainly liberal with largesse; and he showed a personal and practical interest in agriculture which may well have pleased the farming class.

With the subject towns he was no less fortunate. Florence under one was a less tyrannical mistress than under many rulers; their privileges were respected; there were no such incidents as the Volterran Catasto and the consequent revolt during Cosimo's life; their commerce was allowed freer scope; a policy of conciliating Pisa was initiated when the foundations of a new palace were laid in that city.

Cosimo reaped the fruit of a liberal policy in the fidelity shown by the subject towns and even villages in the time of invasion. There were hardly any plots amongst the people in favour of the invaders. We find the most gallant, even heroic, resistance in tiny hill-fortresses, Castel S. Niccolò in 1440, Fojano in 1452, instead of the universal cowardice and treachery which were shown during the Albizzi rule. Piombino, whose ruler, Rinaldo Orsini, was ricommandato to Florence, held out gallantly against Alfonso for several months, and Orsini was duly rewarded afterwards. The Malaspina of the Lunigiana, also ricommandati, and connected by marriage with Lorenzo de' Medici, sent substantial military assistance in the troubles of 1440. Even the behaviour of the Condottieri seemed to improve; perhaps they recognised that they had one strong instead of many weak masters; perhaps they appreciated the fidelity of Florence to Sforza, and thought it worth while to be faithful themselves in the hope of gaining similar rewards.

In the same way, Cosimo skilfully avoided collisions with the smaller independent or semi-independent states which surrounded Florence. The Peace of 1439 with Lucca was strictly preserved; nor did Lucca ever attempt to join in any of the subsequent attacks on Florence. With Perugia a steady league was maintained. Siena, in spite of the hostilities of 1453, on the occasion of the Neapolitan invasion, was conciliated when Florence, after Ferrante's retreat, would not revenge herself for the aid given to him. With Bologna very close relations were maintained, of which some account has already been given. The Bentivogli, who, of all the Italian tyrants, most resembled the Medici in the character and scope of their rule, were on very friendly terms with Cosimo. When their family seemed in danger of extinction, Cosimo sought out a young illegitimate son of Ercole Bentivoglio—Santi—living in obscurity in Florence, and sent him to Bologna to supply the deficiency. Santi remained on intimate terms with the Medici; much correspondence passed between them, in which he continued to declare his gratitude and affection, and Giovanni de' Medici was present at his wedding. Bologna was a steady ally in all the wars after 1441, instead of the constant anxiety which she had been to the Albizzi government.

Certain of Cosimo's personal characteristics were of not a little assistance to him. Not the least of his many gifts was his power of commanding confidence. He was always cool and collected, never flurried or excited; he never lost his temper nor his self-command. When Ferrante's invasion was filling the hearts of the Florentines with terror, and the news that he had captured the village of Rencine was adding to the general panic, Cosimo, with an air of admirable indifference, remarked to the citizen who excitedly told him of its fall: "Ah, indeed! But where *is* Rencine?"

A man of few words, he did not make many promises, but those which he made were always performed, and thus he inspired confidence in all those who had any dealings with him. So highly was his opinion valued that, in spite of the caustic form which it often took, his advice was frequently asked even in the management of domestic affairs.

In spite of their love of amusement the Florentines were, for Italians, a singularly seriously-minded people, and had a great admiration for gravity in others. And Cosimo, we are told, "was much inclined to seriousness, and to consort with great men, far removed from all levity; he hated buffoons, actors, and all those who spent their time uselessly." He himself could certainly never be accused of wasting time. He never played games, "unless it were one game of chess after dinner." When in the country, he would get up early in the morning to work in his garden himself. "He was as avaricious of time as Midas was of gold," said Ficino, the Platonist. "Never idle, never dilatory," wrote Politian, another great scholar, "he does not allow his work to overpower him, and though he has so much business on hand, he actually seems to have nothing to do."

Every moment spared from politics and business was employed in reading or intellectual conversation, to a great extent upon religious subjects. Cosimo was a "great reader of Holy Scripture," and amongst his most intimate friends were the saintly Archbishop of Florence, Antonino, the Camaldulese monk, Ambrogio Traversari, learned in theology, and the mystic painter, Fra Angelico. Cosimo appropriated one of the cells in the convent of S. Marco to his own use, and thither he frequently repaired to meet Angelico or S. Antonino, when the latter was prior of the convent. Another of his friends was Timoteo Maffei, a regular canon of the Monastery of S. Matteo at Fiesole, and in his company Cosimo was in the habit of going into retreat at that monastery for a few days every year.

According to his lights, Cosimo was without doubt a deeply religious man. Nicodemo, who was not in the habit of slurring over the faults of those—Cosimo included—whom he described in his letters to Sforza, laid stress on the reality of his religious belief. No one could have been more munificent in alms-giving to the poor and in endowments to the Church. The convent of S. Marco and that of the Barefooted Friars at Caffaggiuolo, the Badia of Fiesole, the Church of S. Lorenzo and the Noviciate of Sᵃ Croce were all built, and the convents endowed, at his expense. His friend and earliest biographer, the bookseller Vespasiano, gives us a characteristic account of how he came to undertake all this ecclesiastical work. "Cosimo having occupied himself with the temporal affairs of the city, in which it was impossible that he should not have laid some burden on his conscience, as they always must who govern states, and wish to be supreme above others; knowing this, and that, if he hoped for God to have mercy upon him, and to continue to him these temporal advantages, he must turn himself to holy things . . . it seemed to him, I do not know why, that he had money which had not been altogether well acquired. And he asked advice of Pope Eugenius, who was then in Florence, how to lift this load from off his shoulders. Eugenius advised him to build a new convent for the friars of S. Marco, and for the satisfaction and disburdenment of his conscience to spend 10,000 florins on the building. But the whole erection cost him over 40,000." No doubt Cosimo considered, according to the mediæval belief in the atonement of a good deed for a bad one, that with the vast sums of money which he lavished on the Church he was paying a fair price for the ruin and misery of numbers of his fellow-citizens.

In private life Cosimo's morality was certainly not

below that of the day. He had one illegitimate son, the child of a servant, but there were few Florentines who had none, and Carlo was openly acknowledged, brought up in the family on an equality with the legitimate children, and well provided for in an ecclesiastical career. There was never any lack of tender kindliness between Cosimo and all the members of his family; indeed his domestic affection is the most attractive trait in his character. His brother, Lorenzo, and cousin, Bernadetto, were both devoted to him, and followed his lead unquestioningly, even the ambitious Averardo seems to have looked to him as a leader. With his wife he was always tender and kindly, indulgent to the little feminine weakness of the excellent house-wife. In the education of his grandsons he was much interested, anxious that when they should be left alone in the world, which might soon happen, they should be well fortified to meet its difficulties boldly and wisely. If he could have seen Lorenzo a few years later, he would hardly have been disappointed.

A momentary insight is allowed us into the domestic life of Cosimo and his family by the letters of Galeazzo Sforza to his father on the occasion of his visit to Florence. He was much impressed by the friendliness and hospitality of his Medici hosts. Even the ladies of the family, he wrote, were permitted to remain in the room with him, and shared in entertaining him. One of Cosimo's daughters charmed him with her performance on a metal instrument called an " organo di cave." He was enthusiastic in his admiration of the beauties of Careggi, its gardens, furniture and household appointments, even of the excellent cooking. All the family dined with him, except Giovanni, who did not sit down to table in order that he might superintend the serving of the dinner. There were eight gilded dishes upon the table, not including those for sweets. Afterwards a musician played upon the zither,—music was one of Cosimo's few diversions,—and a poet recited verses. Then the company danced, the wives of Piero and Giovanni and Piero's eldest daughter taking part in the dancing, and a collation was served before Galeazzo departed, well pleased with his entertainment.

The wives of Piero and Giovanni were Lucrezia Tornabuoni and Cornelia degli Alessandri; both were from burgher families raised into importance through their adherence to the Medici.

Cosimo's sons were bound to him by the closest ties of familiar affection and respect. It was the death of the younger, Giovanni, in 1463, which hastened his own. Piero's health had always been bad; he suffered constantly from the gout which plagued all the family, and frequently laid up Cosimo himself. Hardly thinking that Piero could long survive him, Cosimo had set his hopes upon Giovanni, as the successor to his position. There was no jealousy between the brothers; Cosimo told Piero that he had never thought it necessary to make a will, "because he always saw us," wrote Piero, "loving and esteeming one another, and agreeing together."

Giovanni's death was therefore a heavy blow, but Cosimo bore it like the philosopher it was his pride to be; "he shed few tears, his voice was steady, and his words were those of a philosopher and a saint." "Nicodemo," he said to the Milanese envoy, "give thyself no trouble to console me; for I should be ashamed not to behave myself in this trouble as I have often admonished you and others to do. I tell you that there are two sorts of men who in such circumstances need consolation; the one are those who do not stand well with our Lord God; the others are those who want self-control." But the blow told heavily, and Cosimo's health failed rapidly from that moment. There is pathos in the picture described to us of the sick old man carried through the spacious halls of the house which he sadly exclaimed was "too large for so small a family."

The curious mixture of Pagan and Christian philosophy so characteristic of the best minds of the age was nowhere better exemplified than in the man who founded the Platonic Academy, "for the reconciliation of Plato and Christianity." Though the ideal reconciliation was unattainable, the practical effect upon the character of those who attempted it was far from unhappy. Cosimo was ready to meet his own death, as he had borne that of his son, "like a philosopher and a saint." Once more to quote his first biographer: "Towards the end of his life Cosimo became very silent, often remaining several hours without speaking, only thinking. One day his wife asked him the reason of this silence, and he answered her, 'When we are going to our country-house, you are busy for a fortnight preparing for the move, but since I have to go from this life to another, does it not seem to you that I ought to have something to think about?'" During the last year of his life he had read to him the *Ethics* of Aristotle, and he was eagerly studying Ficino's translation of Plato, *On the Highest Good.*

It is worth while perhaps to quote Piero's account of his death: "It appeared to me that he grew weaker, and so it seemed to himself, so that on Thursday evening he would have no one in the room but Mona Contessina" (his wife) "and me. He began to recount all his life from the beginning, since he entered upon the government of the city, and then described all his business transactions, and spoke of domestic affairs about the houses and property, and then about you two" (Piero's sons), "counselling me that, as you had good abilities, I ought to bring you up well, since you would then relieve me of many cares. He lamented two things: one not to have done all that he could and would have done; the other that, I being in bad health, he left me with much sorrow. He also said that he did not want any pomp or demonstration at his funeral ... nor more or less wax than is required for an ordinary funeral ... affirming that alms and other good deeds ought to be done as he had done them during life, when they are of more profit than afterwards. ... He reminded me, as he had told me before, of where he wished to be buried in S. Lorenzo, and said all in such an orderly manner, and with so much prudence and spirit, that it was quite marvellous. He added that his life had been long, so that he would leave it well content when God wished. Yesterday morning he had himself dressed completely; he confessed to the prior of S. Lorenzo, and afterwards had mass said, making the responses as if he were in health. Afterwards, being asked to make profession of his faith, he answered word for word, said the confession himself, and received the Holy Sacrament with as much devotion as one can describe, having first asked pardon of every one. Which things have encouraged me in my hope towards God; and, although according to the senses I am not without sorrow, yet, seeing the greatness of his soul and his good disposition, I am in great part content for him."

Piero was not able to comply precisely with the instructions, since all the city flocked to the funeral, and though, according to Cosimo's wish, his tomb was merely a plain slab of porphyry let into the floor before the choir of S. Lorenzo, it was his fellow-citizens who chose the epitaph engraved upon it, "Cosmus Medices hic situs est decreto publico Pater Patriae." Nor is there any doubt that the majority of those who gave Cosimo his posthumous title were quite in earnest in the bestowal of it. The difference between his steady self-control and the passionate instability of Rinaldo degli Albizzi it was easy to appreciate, and the Florentines marked their sense of the distinction by the great trust which, in spite of sundry grumblings, they reposed in Cosimo. Without this confidence, he could never have ruled as he did; and it is in itself the most certain sign that, although he made himself a tyrant, the tyranny was not established over unwilling subjects, nor used, when established, at variance with what the subjects themselves considered to be their own best interests.

A shower of wordy panegyrics were poured out in memory of the great citizen. In one elegiac poem, according to the taste of the time, he was described as being greeted in Heaven by Cicero, who also had been called Pater Patriæ, and being escorted by him and the Fabii, etc., into the company of blameless spirits. But the most notable and weighty is the brief verdict of Rinuccini,—himself an ardent Republican and far from a flatterer of tyrants,—" a wise man, with such wealth and reputation that his equal has never before been seen in our city."

CHAPTER VII

COSIMO'S PATRONAGE OF LITERATURE AND ART

"Those potentates stand highest in the estimation of succeeding ages . . . who have in their own time done honour and given aid and encouragement to that which remains great and memorable in all time." (Letter from James Spedding to Tennyson, quoted in the *Life of Tennyson*.)

IN summing up the characteristics of Cosimo de' Medici's rule in Florence, some, which were perhaps among the most important and to his contemporaries the most evident, have so far been lightly touched upon, because while they are closely connected with political characteristics, they are yet of a slightly different nature and are best treated separately.

The very ground-work upon which Cosimo built up his power was his ability to identify himself closely with the aims and aspirations of his countrymen, and by means of his wealth to assist in the attainment of these ideals, so that he gradually became the representative man in Florence, the man to whom every one looked as pioneer and guide, and to whom every one turned for sympathy, counsel, and assistance. Thus the title of Pater Patriæ was not an idle compliment, but was seriously meant by the majority of the citizens, who really felt towards him as to a father,—the protector of Florence, who obtained for her all that made life worth living, peace, wealth, and culture. Just as he led the way in the commercial world, extending Florentine markets, assisting trading houses, bringing commerce and wealth to the city, so also he led the way in that world of literature and art which, to the fifteenth-century Florentine, was of almost equal importance with the world of trade.

For during the long years of peace under the oligarchy the Florentines had been able to turn their energies to the cultivation of the Renascence spirit which was springing up in their midst. All over Italy the Middle Ages were passing away, and the spirit of mediævalism was growing weaker. It had never indeed had the same power in Italy as over the northern nations. Mysticism, feudalism, chivalry, the absorption of the individual in the community, the art of the Goths and Normans, were none of them native growths; they had all been forced upon Italy from without,—the peculiar characteristics of the north being for a time impressed upon the south. But with the absorption of foreign elements, Lombard or Norman, into the Italian nationality, with the weakening of the Germanic empire, the Italian states gained independence, and the Italian mind, struggling for liberty, shook off the foreign domination. The mediæval religious ideal could not preserve its power over a people so keen and critical, with all its facilities for observing the Papacy at first hand, and with a barely tolerant contempt for the illogical existence of a thoroughly worldly church.

mediæval political ideal, the imperial unity, was hopelessly shattered. The Italian mind did not, like that of the northerner, grope out into the chaos for fresh ideals, fresh systems of religion and politics. With unhesitating, undoubting instinct it threw off the trammels of mediæval thought, and seized upon the remaining fragments of the ancient system of life and culture.

For the civilisation of ancient Rome had taken too deep a root in Italy to be wholly destroyed by mediæval barbarism. The traces of antique culture, and of a wide, scientific and self-conscious mode of thought were never wholly effaced from the minds of the Italians. They still looked upon what Rome had been and done as the national title to glory. Latin literature was widely if not deeply known. The fragments of Roman architecture and sculpture still existed to point to what had once been. The Renascence, which was an artificial creation in the northern nations, was in Italy only the re-awakening of a sleeping spirit. Yet the Italian culture of the fifteenth century was not wholly modelled upon the antique. It was to the study of nature and of man that the Italians, when emancipated from mediævalism, gave their active interest. They discovered anew the beauty of the outward world, the fascination of the study of human character and thought. Subjectively they became conscious of their individuality, objectively they learned to look upon their surroundings with the delighted interest of children in a newly-discovered playground. Antique thought, based itself upon nature, was the best guide to nature, and on the artistic side of Italian culture it never was more than a guide, though in literature, in Cosimo's time at least, it became an object of somewhat slavish imitation.

So absorbing were the new interests, and so fascinating their pursuit, that the great fundamental questions which racked Europe in the fifteenth and sixteenth centuries were passed over in Italy as little more than exercises in mental gymnastics. The religious battle was hardly more than a wordy squabble; the political and social strifes took the form of sham wars between petty states, and wranglings amongst a few ambitious characters for a transitory predominance in which the mass of the people took very little interest. Even Florence, where political life existed long after it was dead elsewhere, suffered herself to be soothed to sleep under the Medici spell, and accepted their domination with less and less resistance, caring little by whom she was ruled so long as she was enabled to indulge the growing passion for wealth, art, and literature, the increasing luxury and fulness of her physical life. She had had enough of faction-fighting, of house-burnings and street murders, she wanted peace and leisure for the new pursuits, and these under the Medici she obtained.

Florence was herself indeed the pioneer of the Renascence. From Florence it spread over Italy, and thence to the rest of Europe, but in Florence it had its origin, and attained there its highest development. Tuscany had from the first suffered less from Trans-Alpine interference than the rest of Italy, and Florence looked upon herself both in politics and culture as the heir of ancient Rome. In Florence, free institutions and the constant shiftings of the political world gave scope for the development of individuality. The Florentine character was, like that of the ancient Athenians, distinguished for its keenness, eagerness, restlessness, mental activity, its creative and critical faculties, constantly interacting upon each other, and particularly for its delicate æsthetic taste and its over-mastering passion for the beautiful. As in Athens, the national institutions and national character combined to produce that marvellous efflorescence of the human mind which in one case we call the Athenian, in the other the Florentine, culture.

Even before the revival of antiquity Florence was already the home of the best literature and art in Italy. She had produced Dante, Petrarch, and Boccaccio, Arnolfo, Giotto, and Orcagna. The tradition was passed on from generation to generation; the artist and savant grew up in an atmosphere of culture, shared in the conquests over technical difficulties made by their predecessors, and inherited that love of the beautiful, tempered with a fine, critical taste, which produced the peculiar quality and essence of the best Florentine minds, its delicacy and freshness, its refinement and reserve. Her free political life encouraged that patriotism which formed so large an element in her literary and artistic enthusiasms. While Dante was expounded to the people in the Cathedral on Saints' Days, the official Government, the Guilds and the richer families vied with one another in storing the city with objects of beauty, to make her the loveliest of Italian towns,— "the joy of the whole earth." The Signory provided monuments for public men in the churches, the Art of Wool undertook the building of the Cathedral, that of the Merchants procured the bronze doors for the

Baptistry; the Strozzi, Pazzi and Pitti amongst other leading families built and adorned palaces, restored or decorated churches.

Social conditions also favoured the development. The lines of class distinction had never been so deeply drawn as in feudalistic countries; the common interests of the Renascence drew classes still closer together; talent, wherever found, could make itself known. The great burghers took pride and pleasure in patronising it; they even entered the literary arena themselves, though the practice of art was still considered a handicraft in which they could not take part with dignity. The political leaders were amongst the most prominent of patrons. Palla Strozzi was on the University Board; it was mainly owing to his exertions that the Greek, Manuel Chrysoloras, was, at the end of the fourteenth century, brought to Florence to teach his native language there. Palla collected books, amongst them some in Greek; he purposed to found a Public Library; Tommaso Parentucelli, afterwards the famous humanist and patron of learning, Pope Nicolas V., was tutor to his sons. It is not surprising, therefore, to find that Cosimo's interest in contemporary learning and art preceded in point of time the development of his political ambitions. A thorough Florentine in character, his taste and sympathies led him to assume the position of a Mæcenas. Well educated, with a sufficient knowledge of Latin and some acquaintance with Greek, he read in ancient literature as then known, with a fine æsthetic taste, and a deep interest in all the questions of the day, particularly in those of abstract philosophy, he combined with these qualities a natural liberality inspired not only by political interests, but by a genuine love of the culture he patronised, by the instinct of an enthusiastic curio-collector and by a real passion for bricks and mortar. As a collector he had exceptional opportunities. The Medici banking-firm had branch houses and agents in every part of the known world, and especially in the East, where Greek books and art treasures could be obtained. They had orders to purchase, regardless of expense, everything that they could lay hands on, and accordingly, even before the date of his exile, Cosimo had a fine collection of MSS., Latin and Greek, of coins, medals, vases, cameos, jewels and fragments of statuary, which his wealth had often enabled him to purchase over the heads of other bidders. When in 1430 he went to Verona to escape from the plague, he was accompanied by his friends, Niccolò Niccoli, and Carlo d'Arezzo, two of the most notable literary men of the day; and, during his exile in Venice, he had with him the architect, Michelozzo Michelozzi, who built there at Cosimo's expense the Library of S. Giorgio as a mark of gratitude to his Venetian hosts.

Cosimo's personal predilections, therefore, were in harmony with the object that he had set before himself, to take the first place in the best Florentine society, which at that moment was absorbed in the æsthetic and literary movement, and use this as a basis for the extension of his political influence. To him "poet, classical scholar and artist were all links in one chain,"[1] the chain which bound Florence to himself. "Those whom he rewarded and recompensed hardly knew whether they had to thank Cosimo, Pater Patriæ, or

---

[1] Voigt, *Die Wiederlebung des classischen Alterthums.*

Cosimo, the private citizen."[1] Thus, without assuming the title of ruler, he assumed that place in society which at Naples was occupied by the King, at Ferrara and Urbino by the Dukes. The influence of the most highly cultivated minds was on his side; his wealth was lavished on the adornment of the city by buildings, sculpture and painting, and not less by the men of learning who were attracted thither by his patronage. To reckon the great Mæcenas as a fellow-citizen was an honour in itself. While employment was given to great numbers of the poor upon his buildings, the religious sentiments still very strong amongst the uneducated and even some of the educated classes were gratified, and his own conscience was salved, by his liberality towards the Church in buildings and endowments.

The Renascence passion for posthumous fame pushed him onwards. The praises of great scholars in their writings, the tangible works of stone and marble would alone, he believed, give him that immortality for which he, in common with his contemporaries, most craved. In less than fifty years, he himself had said, nothing of him nor of his house should be found in Florence but these few buildings of his.

The expenditure of his wealth upon such objects he felt to be the most profitable of his investments, even more so than the buying up of personal adherents with pecuniary favours. His liberality astonished his contemporaries, and many stories were told of his seemingly reckless generosity. We hear how one of his bank managers, making up accounts, found that 7000 florins had been spent in that year alone on building the Badia

[1] Voigt, *Die Wiederlebung des classischen Alterthums.*

and S. Lorenzo. "Thinking to frighten Cosimo," he hastened to inform him of this extravagance. The answer was somewhat disconcerting. "I understand you!" Cosimo said; "the builders of S. Lorenzo deserve severe blame for not having done more work, and those of the Badia merit praise for their superior industry." Again, we hear how Cosimo made up to the contractor who undertook the building of Careggi some money which he had spent over and above the contract. This generosity was not always unprofitable, even from a pecuniary point of view. As a reward for liberal loans to him when Bishop of Bologna, Nicolas V. made Cosimo Papal banker, from which employment he reaped large profits.

With awe-struck wonder the Florentines told of the 400,000 gold florins Cosimo was said to have spent in taxes, charities and public buildings alone—a sum which would have paid the expenses of a war for six years, and which probably only included a fraction of all that he disbursed, if there are included his private subsidies to State expenses and secret-service money, his assistance of other business firms and of literary and artistic men, public festivals, the entertainment of distinguished visitors, the purchase of books, pictures and other objects of art, the latter of which alone were worth nearly 40,000 ducats. The astonishing speed with which he made and spent money, we can gather from the fact that his fortune at the time of his father's death was less than 200,000 florins; he spent this sum many times over on what we may call public objects alone. It was private economy which in a large measure enabled him to do this. Nothing unnecessary was spent on his own indulgence, on luxurious living, amusement or personal adornment. The expenditure on books, on objects of art, for his private library and private dwelling-house, were in a sense public, since the library was open to his scholar friends, the art-collection to the artists. The antique fragments of statuary in his garden were studied by young sculptors as if in a public school of art.

The Medici Palace in the Via Larga became the centre of intellectual, as well as of political life in Florence. Here men of learning gathered to discuss the literary and philosophic questions of the day, and hither all distinguished visitors to the city repaired to meet them. Cosimo was capable of conversing with each upon his special subject, and his keen judgment enabled him to criticise all that was said, and to form a correct estimate of the speakers. With many of them he formed close and enduring friendships; and it is some proof of his attractiveness that these friends were very diverse in character and interests.

Dearest amongst them was Niccolò Niccoli, of whom mention has already been made as accompanying Cosimo to Verona in 1430. He might almost be described as Florentine Minister for Literature and Education from about 1400 until his death in 1437, and though his power was diminished during Cosimo's exile, it was restored on his return. He was Literary Dictator and Oracle in Florence; his criticism upon Latin style was considered almost final. But so fastidious was his taste that he was never sufficiently satisfied with his own productions to publish them, and the sharpness of his criticisms involved him in quarrels with most of his literary contemporaries. To youthful seekers after learning he was, however, always encouraging and helpful, particularly by freely lending his many valuable books. He and Palla Strozzi practically managed the University of Florence, securing for it many Greek teachers, first Manuel Chrysoloras, and afterwards several Italians who had studied in Constantinople, and returned thence with much learning and a great store of classical manuscripts. Each of these men was in turn driven to leave Florence, mainly on account of quarrels with the peppery Niccoli, who wished to criticise them and dictate to them as if they were his pupils. Yet the study of Greek flourished in Florence, and it was mainly owing to her patronage of Greek teachers and purchase of their books that most at least of what was best in ancient Greek literature had found its way to Italy, before the fall of Constantinople obliterated its last traces in the Eastern Empire.

The collection of ancient manuscripts, hidden for many generations in old libraries, particularly in the monasteries, neglected, forgotten, often half-destroyed, was one of the first and principal labours of the early humanists. In this work Niccoli was a keen enthusiast, and the resources of Cosimo's wealth were open to him for this purpose. The Medici agents, who were charged, beyond their financial business, with the work of collecting books and antiques, were under his direction. We find him sending orders through Cosimo that a unique copy of Livy should be purchased from a monastery at Lübeck. Niccoli was also in intimate correspondence with numerous independent book-collectors. They lent him the manuscripts which they discovered, and he copied them himself, collecting

altogether a library of eight hundred books, a [very]
large number for that time, most of which were [in his]
own hand-writing. His private fortune, wh[ich was]
small, was soon exhausted in the purchase of b[ooks and]
antiquities; that he might live comfortably and co[ntinue]
his work without hindrance, Cosimo gave orde[rs to his]
banking-houses that all drafts made upon th[em by]
Niccoli should be freely honoured. Cosimo's g[enerosity]
was rewarded when the whole of Niccoli's fine l[ibrary]
fell into his hands at the owner's death. The l[egacy]
was employed according to the wishes of the tes[tator.]
During Niccoli's lifetime, his books had practi[cally]
constituted a public library for all who wished to [read]
them. The greater part of them, therefore, Cosi[mo]
established in the newly-built convent of S. Marco,
where they were free to all students, and formed [the]
nucleus of the first Public Library in Florence, a[nd]
in modern Europe. Since Niccoli's books were a[lmost]
entirely classical, Cosimo added many others from [his]
private collection, or bought for the purpose. To his oth[er]
religious foundations also Cosimo presented librar[ies;]
the most noted of these was that of the Badia at F[iesole.]
Finding it impossible to buy, without a very long d[elay,]
all the books required for this library, Cosimo ga[ve]
directions to the bookseller, Vespasiano, to emp[loy]
writers for the transcription of all that were need[ed.]
In twenty-two months two hundred volumes were t[hus]
transcribed by the forty-five copyists whom Vespasi[ano]
set to work. The catalogue was drawn up by Tom[maso]
Parentucelli, and served as a model for many oth[er]
great Italian collections. These libraries of Cos[imo,]
together with his valuable private collection of bo[oks,]

formed at a later date the germ of the famous Laurentian Library, and are to be found in it to this day.

Noted amongst the book-collectors was another of Cosimo's friends, hardly less intimate than Niccoli, Ambrogio Traversari. He was a Camaldulese monk, and became general of his order. In the exercise of this office he had many opportunities for discovering manuscripts, and all that he found he brought to Florence, and shared with his friends. His good nature and cheerfulness made him as much loved by his literary contemporaries as Niccoli was feared. His cell at the Camaldulese Monastery of S^a Maria degli Angeli was one of the regular resorts of literary society; and here Cosimo might often be found amongst the rest, listening to Traversari's translation of the Epistles of St. Paul, which Niccoli took down from his dictation, or conversing on theological subjects, for Traversari contrived to keep clear of the Paganistic tendencies of classical learning, and never forgot that he was a monk and a theologian, however much he might find pleasure in classical authors. He made it a rule to confine his translations from the Greek, which were his principal contributions to literature, to Scripture and the works of the Christian fathers. Once he broke this rule at Cosimo's request, only to regret bitterly that his friendship had led him away from the path his conscience had marked out.

Neither Niccoli nor Traversari produced original work of any importance. The leaders of literary production in Florence were the successive Florentine chancellors, who were all selected for that office as brilliant Latin stylists. They employed the Ciceronian Latin, then fashionable, in the State documents which they drew up, and in the public orations which it was frequently their duty to make for the Signory. The three most noted men who held the Chancery during Cosimo's rule were Lionardo Bruni (1427-44), Carlo Marsuppini (1444-53), and Poggio Bracciolini (1453-58). They all came originally from Arezzo, all learned secretarial work in the Papal Curia, and all having gained their enthusiasm for learning in Florence, made her their adopted home. "I must visit Florence at least once a year," wrote Poggio from Rome. To each the Florentine Chancery was the object of his highest ambition.

Literary talent seems instinctively to have ranged itself on the Medicean side in politics, since Bruni, having once or twice tried in vain to obtain the Chancery, at last received it when the Medici turned out Paolo Fortini (1427). Bruni might have suffered in 1433, but that he had opportunely quarrelled with Niccoli, and probably on that account was allowed to retain his position. Bruni's quarrel with Niccoli was not, however, extended to Cosimo, whose social position placed him above mere literary squabbles. So far as Bruni's somewhat morose character would permit, he and Cosimo always remained friends. In Florence Bruni's chief fame rested upon his monumental History of the Republic, which, as her chief literary official, Bruni considered it his special duty to undertake. Composed after the model of Latin history, it flattered the patriotic sentiments of the Florentines by the parallel it suggested between their city and ancient Rome. Bruni was rewarded by immunity from taxation, and by a grand state funeral. The volumes of his history were laid upon his breast as his body was carried upon an open bier in procession through the city, an oration was delivered over him, and his brows were crowned with laurel. His successor, Marsuppini, was also, like Bruni, a proud and reserved man, and had no friends outside the circle of the Medici, but with them he was on intimate terms. His reputation lay rather in his lectures on rhetoric and Greek at the University than in his literary work; but he, like Bruni, received a public funeral and coronation with the poet's laurel.

Poggio Bracciolini is one of the most characteristic figures of the Renascence of learning, and at the same time one of those most closely connected with Cosimo. There is no room here for an account of his literary industries and enthusiasms, his personal collection of manuscripts in all parts of Europe, even in England, the use of which he freely shared with Niccoli and his friends in Florence, his vast literary production, and his numerous literary quarrels. Poggio possessed a particularly neat and caustic style of prose, and no one knew better how to make a sarcasm sting. Many of these quarrels were on subjects of purely academic interest, such as a comparison of the merits of Cæsar and Scipio, though even such a seemingly unimportant question led the opponents, after the fashion of the time, to make the most shameless aspersions upon one another's private character.

But the principal quarrel in which Poggio was involved had rather a political than literary interest, and Cosimo himself was deeply concerned in it. As a member of the Papal Curia Poggio accompanied Eugenius IV. to Florence in 1433, and here he found ready all the materials for a very promising battle with the most noted and formidable humanist of the age, Francesco Filelfo. Niccoli had invited Filelfo to teach Greek at the Florentine University; and as Filelfo was as conceited and boastful as he was learned, the usual quarrel soon broke out, in which all the humanists in Florence were speedily involved. Niccoli, being the special protégé of Cosimo, Filelfo speedily identified his interests with those of the Albizzi, and thus the battle came to be fought on political lines. Filelfo was in correspondence with the Milanese Government, and declared that he had received information of the supposed intrigue between Cosimo and Visconti. An attempt was made to assassinate Filelfo, which he believed to have been prompted by the Medici. Cosimo's imprisonment was therefore Filelfo's triumph. He wrote to the Signory urging that the prisoner should not escape with his life, and bitterly reproached Palla Strozzi for the faintheartedness which condemned Cosimo to exile only. On Cosimo's return, Filelfo, soon finding Florence too hot to hold him, retired to Siena, and a formal sentence of banishment was pronounced against him. Another attempt was made to assassinate Filelfo in Siena, and he retaliated by sending a hired assassin to Florence to murder Cosimo and Niccoli. Filelfo was declared a rebel, and condemned to lose his tongue if he were caught.

But he was in possession of a sharper weapon than the assassin's knife. "Cosimo brought poison and dagger against me," he said, "and I will bring my mind and pen against him." He accordingly wrote *The Book of Exile*, in which the victims of 1434 were made to appear and give their opinions. It was full of the most violent and unmeasured abuse against the Medici and their friends, including Niccoli and Poggio. Poggio was the only man capable of a suitable reply. The invective which he launched against Filelfo exceeded Filelfo's own work in its virulence and abusiveness. The most horrible accusations were made against Filelfo and all his relations, of which the theft of books and jewels was one of the most moderate. Filelfo replied in verse, heaping insults upon Poggio, and the quarrel continued with intervals until 1447. Filelfo took refuge in Milan, and was hand and glove with the exiles; but as early as 1437 he was attempting to return to Florence, where, after all, he had found himself most comfortable, and where alone he could procure the books that he needed. He issued a manifesto to the people of Florence in favour of the exiles, but no notice was taken of it. In 1440 he was encouraging Rinaldo in the invasion which ended in the battle of Anghiari, and at the same moment he was making conciliatory offers to Cosimo himself. These he renewed a few years later, writing flattering letters to Cosimo's two sons in hopes of their mediation, offering "to suppress as far as possible" *The Book of Exile*, even writing a "Cosmias," a poetical panegyric upon Cosimo full of the most fulsome adulation. But, although Sforza offered his mediation, Cosimo never relented, and it was not till Lorenzo's time that Filelfo was allowed to return to die in Florence.

In spite of Poggio's services, he was already seventy-three years old when he reached the height of his ambition and became Chancellor of Florence. He was glad to be settled amongst his old friends, and he undertook the completion of Bruni's History of the Republic, but he found the weight of office too heavy for him, and soon resigned.

Once at least, in his persecution of Giannozzo Manetti, Cosimo allowed political to outweigh literary considerations. Manetti, while not producing original literary work of any value, was a perfect storehouse of all the learning attainable at the time. His studies even embraced Hebrew, and his deepest interest was in theological controversy with the Jews. Perhaps Cosimo thought Manetti too clever, certainly he had gained a reputation for brilliant oratory which made him over-conspicuous in a city where Cosimo wished every one but himself to be equal. Since books were scarce and public festivals plentiful, oratory had become of very great importance. Every possible opportunity, the reception of distinguished visitors, the complimentary visits of ambassadors, the installation of a new official, a public funeral, was seized upon to make speeches, often some hours in length, and, to our taste, infinitely wearisome, since they consisted of little but strings of platitudes, loaded with classical quotations; but they were listened to eagerly by people who thought more of style than of matter, and were never weary of hearing the classics quoted. It was not without reason that Italian ambassadors were commonly called "Orators."

Cosimo patronised Marsuppini as a rival orator to Manetti, and, on the state reception of Frederick III, arranged that he should have the honour of welcoming the Emperor. But they had not counted upon the eloquence of Frederick's secretary, Æneas Sylvius (after wards Pope Pius II.), whose speech of reply itself required an answer. Marsuppini declared that he could not speak unprepared, and the Signory, much embarrassed, had to fall back upon Manetti, whose extempore speech was afterwards declared to have been better than Marsuppini's elaborately prepared oration.

It was in the study of Greek philosophy, however, that Cosimo personally took a deeper interest than in any other branch of learning. This interest was awakened by the Platonist revival, which followed on the importation of Greek books, and especially the works of the Neo-Platonists, into Italy in the early part of the fifteenth century. Aristotelian philosophy, more or less distorted by the schoolmen, had been widely known in the Middle Ages, while Plato was to the fifteenth-century Italian almost a new discovery. The presence of all the most learned men of Greece at the Council of Florence in 1439 gave a new impulse to the study of Greek; and amongst them was Gemistos Plethon, a philosopher who believed that the mantle of Plato had descended upon himself. He inspired the higher minds in Florence with his own passion for Plato. Curiously enough, it was Cosimo, the practical burgher and cynical politician, whose mind might have been expected to be rather materialistic than visionary, who, more than any one else, fell under the spell of Plato's mystic idealism. His devotion to Plato henceforward coloured all his life, and became a passion hardly second to his desire for political absolutism. He taught his friends to think with him, and set the fashion of a Plato worship, which soon became the dominating note of literary society in Florence. Cosimo founded a "Platonic Academy," which met at his house at Careggi to discuss philosophical questions. Here the best minds of the day came together in intellectual contest, and Cosimo himself took a not unimportant part in all the discussions.

To make Plato really popular, however, it was necessary that he should be completely translated. Cosimo was not satisfied with the earlier translations, and conceived the plan of educating his protégé, Marsiglio Ficino, a lad of unusual intelligence, for this purpose alone. When the young man's mind had been sufficiently saturated with Platonic philosophy, he was provided with a house in Florence and a small estate at Careggi, in order that he might be hindered by no material wants, and was set to work. In the year of Cosimo's death he finished the first instalment of the translation, the *De Summo Bono*. Cosimo, lying sick at Careggi, asked him to visit him there. "Come to us, Marsiglio," he wrote, "as soon as you can. Bring with you your translation of Plato *On the Highest Good*. For I desire nothing so much as to learn that road which leads to the highest happiness. Farewell, and come not without thine Orpheus lyre." Ficino warmly acknowledged his indebtedness to Cosimo. "I had two fathers," he wrote, "one Ficino, the Doctor (*Medico*), who brought me into the world, the other Cosimo de' *Medici*, who gave me new life." "I owe to Plato much, to Cosimo no less. He realised for me the virtues of which Plato gave me the conception."

Again, it was Cosimo who invited the Greek, Argyropulos, to Florence in 1456, where he became the teacher of Piero de' Medici, and afterwards of his son, Lorenzo. He and Cosimo were always on the best of terms. On feast days he would go, accompanied by his scholars, to discuss philosophy at the Medici Palace. On Cosimo's death he wrote to Piero, "Where is now our father? Where is our light? Where is the prince and friend of our studies?" It was, therefore, largely due to Cosimo's exertions that, a few years later, Politian could say to the Florentines, "It was in your State, men of Florence, that all Greek culture, which in Greece itself had long been extinguished, awoke and blossomed once more; so that there are men amongst you who teach Greek literature publicly, and the children of your best families, as has not happened for a thousand years in Italy, speak the Attic tongue correctly and easily; so that Athens seems as if it had not been destroyed and taken by the barbarians, but, with all its means of culture, had freely transplanted itself to Florence."

Next, after the study of Platonism, building was Cosimo's special hobby, and in this he was typical of his contemporaries. The increased security of life both within and without the city led to the substitution of palaces and villas for the old fortified dwelling-houses, while church and convent building was always in fashion, even among people who reviled the Church. Cosimo's first care was to complete the rebuilding of the church of S. Lorenzo, which his father had begun. S. Lorenzo was to become the shrine of the Medici family; Cosimo himself is buried before the choir. The architect was Brunelleschi, creator of the marvellous dome of the cathedral, and inventor of fifteenth-century ecclesiastical architecture; S. Lorenzo was one of his masterpieces. The cloisters of the Badia at Fiesole, which he also built for Cosimo, were hardly less successful.

Brunelleschi was the architect of the Pitti Palace; but Cosimo refused his design for the Medici Palace, and accepted the less ambitious plans of Michelozzo Michelozzi, his personal friend and his companion in exile. If Brunelleschi was the church builder, Michelozzo was the builder of palaces and villas *par excellence*. He provided them with handsome exteriors, and comfortable, roomy interiors, convenient for the accommodation of a large household, where there was much going and coming of guests, and suitable to be settings for the exquisite gems of art which were collected within them. No less happy were Cosimo's own villa at Careggi and the conventual buildings of S. Marco, with its graceful, spacious cloister, vaulted chapter-house, convenient dormitories and long, airy library. S. Marco's was the religious house in which Cosimo took most particular interest, and of which his personal friends, the Prior S. Antonino and Fra Angelico, were members.

Cosimo's buildings were not confined to Florence. Erected as compliments to foreign states were the Library of S. Giorgio at Venice, and, in return for the honorary citizenship of that town, the Palazzo Vismara at Milan. The "Florentine College" at Paris,—the dwelling and Guild-House of Merchants from Florence,—was restored, and so also was the Hospital of the Knights of S. John at Acre. Benozzo Gozzoli certainly showed discernment when, in his fresco of the Tower of Babel, he represented Cosimo as superintending the building. But without doubt Cosimo has obtained the reward for which he craved. Now that the dynasty which he founded exists only as an historical memory, his name at least will long be kept alive in connection with those buildings with which he associated it.

Nor was it sufficient that his palaces and villas and churches should be beautiful as buildings alone; they must be decorated within, not only with the fragments of ancient art which he had collected, but also with all that was best in the production of contemporary artists. The walls of his rooms were hung with rich tapestries, some of which were executed at Bruges from cartoons designed in Florence for the purpose; the iron and bronze work and silver plate were of the finest workmanship; the books had the most magnificent bindings and illuminations; the furniture was painted by Dello Delli, who was noted for his skill in this kind of work. Luca della Robbia decorated a summer-house with painted terra-cotta tiles or reliefs. All the resources of sculpture and painting were also called forth in the work of decoration. Ghiberti, the earliest of Renascence sculptors, was too busily engaged upon the wonderful bronze doors of the Baptistry for him to spare much thought for lesser work, yet he found time to set a rare Cornelian for Giovanni de' Medici, and to make a reliquary for Cosimo. But it was Donatello who, among all the artists of the day, was Cosimo's dearest friend and most faithful servant. Their common admiration for classical art, under the influence of which a great deal of Donatello's best work was done, tended to draw them together in sympathy. The eight medallions, with which Donatello decorated the courtyard of the Medici Palace, were direct copies from antique gems in Cosimo's possession. It was Donatello who first suggested to Cosimo the idea of a collection of antiques, and he was largely concerned in its formation and arrangement. He was indeed an antiquarian of no mean capabilities; "Donatello saw it, and praised it highly," was to Poggio Bracciolini a sufficient recommendation of the merits of an ancient work of art. His house was one of the favourite resorts of learned and cultivated society; an unusual honour in an age when the artist was still looked upon as a mere craftsman. Cosimo and he were bound together by the closest ties of friendship, of generosity on the one hand and of gratitude on the other. Cosimo sometimes obtained commissions for Donatello, sometimes stood between him and extortionate employers, who might have imposed upon his well-known unworldliness. Cosimo upbraided Donatello for the slovenliness of his dress, and yet was not offended when Donatello sent back to him his present of a red cloak as too smart for a simple sculptor's wear. The climax of his generosity was a regular provision for Donatello and four workmen, in order that he might be relieved from all anxiety about the necessaries of life. This was followed by a pension from Piero de' Medici; but Donatello died immediately after his old patron, and was buried, at his own request, close to his tomb in S. Lorenzo. Our only regret is that he has not left us a statue or bust of Cosimo. His masterly skill in portraiture, and his wonderful *intimité* with each of his models, would, as in the portraits he made of Niccolò Uzzano, Poggio Bracciolini, and Pope John XXIII. have enabled him to render Cosimo's character with extraordinary force and insight, and the result would have been full of interest.

Amongst the painters, Cosimo's special protégé was the lively and inconsequent friar, Filippo Lippi, the continuator of Masaccio's work on a lower spiritual plane, the embodiment of all that was gayest and most mundane in the Renascence, the child of earth, full of a naïve delight in the charms of the natural world, in the pleasantness of youth and springtime, careless of higher meanings or deeper problems. Cosimo treated him as the man treats the clever, spoilt child, extricating him from his serious scrapes, procuring from the Pope the dispensation for his marriage with Lucrezia Buti, and, when Lippi proved too troublesome, and altogether too casual in the execution of the commissions with which Cosimo had charged him, making him lodge in the Medici Palace until the work was accomplished. "One must treat these people of extraordinary genius as if they were celestial spirits, and not like beasts of burden," Cosimo said, with characteristically tolerant sarcasm. Filippo Lippi painted numerous pictures for him, amongst them the famous little "Madonna" in the Uffizi Gallery, where the young Lorenzo de' Medici figures as a boy-angel.

Of a somewhat similar type, though without its touch of sensuality, was the art of a favourite of Cosimo's later years, Benozzo Gozzoli, whose happiest work was done in depicting country scenes and pleasant landscapes. He was entrusted with the fresco decoration of the chapel in the Medici Palace, and nothing could be more characteristic, both of himself and of his age. It represents the journey of the Magi. All round the walls ride in an unbroken cavalcade the kings and their attendants, a gay and motley crowd, like the throng of a mediæval pilgrimage, arrayed in the brightest and most fanciful of Renascence costume, with hawks and hounds and finely caparisoned horses, yet with something of seriousness in their faces, as if in tribute to the sacred spot in which they find themselves. Beyond them spreads a wide landscape full of enchanting details, a hunt, a group of horsemen, a castellated house upon the hill-top, palm-trees or cypresses. It is impossible to quarrel with anything so fresh, so naïve and yet so sincere, because the artist has treated a great historical subject in the *genre* style, because the kings and their followers are portraits of the Emperor and Patriarch of Constantinople and their suite, of the Medici and their friends, including the artist himself, in contemporary dress, because in fact the religious aspects of the subject are lost sight of, and it is used merely as an excuse for painting what the Italians call a "Trionfo," —the glorification of a person or family, in this case the family whose house it decorated. Cosimo rides in the procession, a soberly attired, unassuming old man, but without the look of foxey cunning which his best known portrait gives him; the lad Lorenzo, crowned with roses, sits jauntily upon his white horse.

As in sculpture, so also Cosimo showed a special interest in the efforts of the painters to construct, partially on classical lines and partially by their own discoveries, a correct system of technique and a realism in treatment to which their study of nature inevitably led them, so that Paolo Uccelli, as well as Donatello, shared in his patronage. Paolo, the aim of whose life was to master the technical difficulties of foreshortening and perspective, was naturally far from attaining a high level of art; yet his work was very valuable in his own time, since it was largely by his struggles and failures that the greater Quattrocentists obtained their absolute mastery over the technique with which he wrestled. Uccelli had also a genuine interest in animal life; we are told that the frescoes with which he decorated the interior of the Medici Palace consisted of scenes in which animals were not merely accessories, but played the principal parts. Andrea del Castagno was still more of a realist than Uccelli. He was a peasant-lad, and his talents were first discovered by Bernadetto de' Medici, who had him educated as an artist. It was he who painted the caricature portraits of the rebels of 1440 upon the walls of the Palazzo Vecchio.

Cosimo has been accused of caring only for what was least elevated in contemporary art, for encouraging realism unduly at the expense of idealism. This charge is refuted by his well-known friendship for the greatest of Quattrocentist idealists, Fra Angelico. In him a strong inborn tendency to mysticism and religious devotion had been fostered by the special teaching of the order to which he belonged, which was strongly conservative in matters of art, and looked upon painting as a direct act of worship,—"a powerful means of elevating the soul and developing holy thoughts in the heart." Angelico most thoroughly believed all that he painted, and experienced himself the religious emotions which he intended to call up in the heart of the spectator. He did not indeed wholly escape from the tendencies of the age, his technique is superior to that of the Trecentists and it improved in his later years, yet to him it always occupied a place quite secondary to the moral meaning which his picture was intended to convey. To Angelico was very naturally entrusted the decoration with religious frescoes of the newly erected Convent of S. Marco, and in this work a great part of his life was spent. The grand Crucifixion in the chapter-house, with its group of representative saints at the foot of the Cross (amongst them SS. Lorenzo and Cosimo, the patrons of the Medici), is perhaps the apotheosis of the ascetic ideal as embodied in pictorial art. It was Angelico's brother, Fra Benedetto, who executed with most exquisite miniatures the choir-books which Cosimo had provided for the use of the convent church.

It was Cosimo's friendliness towards the artists whom he patronised that made him so perfect a patron. While most people looked upon artists merely as highly skilled artisans, he admitted them into his family circle, and between him and them there was what was called "domesticanza." His sons shared his artistic interests and friends. Piero took over the management of the art-collection some time before his father's death. Benozzo Gozzoli called him his "most singular friend," and, when decorating the Medici Palace, wrote to Piero, urging him to return from the country in order to criticise what had already been completed. Another artist we find writing to Giovanni to recommend to his notice a rich young lady as a suitable wife. Carlo de' Medici we hear of in Rome, disputing with the powerful Cardinal Barbo (afterwards Paul II.) over the spoils of the valuable collection left by the great medallist, Pisanello.

In spite of his cold manner and cynical wit, it is plain that there was nothing which Cosimo understood better than the art of popularity. He was popular with all that was highest and best in the intellectual life of the day, with which he was deeply in sympathy.; and, next to the commerce by which they existed, it was with their intellectual pursuits, not with the occasional political storms which broke over them, that the Florentines were most occupied. Cosimo's wisdom taught him how to identify himself with all their interests, to make himself appear to his fellow-citizens as the Florentine amongst Florentines, the "pillar, fountain and banner" of the State, the "father of his country."

APPENDIX

THE following is a list of the principal authorities consulted:—

Albizzi. *Commissioni di Rinaldo degli Albizzi per il Comune di Firenze dal 1399 al 1433.* (*Documenti di storia Italiana.* Firenze, 1867-73.)

Ammirato. *Dell' istorie Fiorentine.* (Firenze, 1641-47.)

Armstrong, E. *Lorenzo de' Medici and Florence in the Fifteenth Century.* (New York and London, 1896.)

Bisticci, Vespasiano da. *Vite di uomini illustri del secolo XV.* (Bologna, 1892.)

Buoninsegni. *Storie della città di Firenze dall' anno 1410 al 1460.* (Firenze, 1637.)

Burckhardt. *Die Cultur der Renaissance in Italien.* (Leipzig, 1869.)

Buser. *Die Beziehungen der Mediceer zu Frankreich während die Jahre 1434-1494 in ihrem Zusammenhang mit den allgemeinen Verhältnissen Italiens.* (Leipzig, 1879.)

Cambi. *Istorie.* (Vols. XX.-XXIII. of *Delizie degli Eruditi Toscani*, pubbl. da Ildefonso di San Luigi. Firenze, 1785.)

Canestrini. *Négociations diplomatiques de la France avec la Toscane.* (Paris, 1857-72.)

Capponi, Gino. *Storia della Repubblica di Firenze.* (Firenze, 1875.)

Capponi, Neri. *Continuatio monumentorum historicorum de rebus Florentinorum Gino Capponi.* (In Vol. XVIII. of *Scriptt. rer. Italicarum*, ed. Muratori, Mediol., 1731.)

Cavalcanti. *Istorie Fiorentine.* (Firenze, 1838, 1839.)

Crowe and Cavalcaselle. *A new History of Painting in Italy.* (London, 1864-66.)

Fabronius. *Magni Cosmi Medicei vita.* (Pisis, 1789.)

Gaspary. *Geschichte der Italienischen Literatur.* (Berlin, Gräfenhainichen, 1885.)

Guicciardini. *Opere inedite.* (Firenze, 1857-63.)

Janitschek. *Die Gesellschaft der Renaissance in Italien und die Kunst.* (Stuttgart, 1879.)

Machiavelli. *Historie Fiorentine.* (Ed. Niccolini, Firenze, 1882.)

Morelli. *Ricordi fatti in Firenze.* (Vol. XIX. of *Delizie degli Eruditi Toscani*, pubbl. da Ildefonso di San Luigi, Firenze, 1785.)

Müntz. *Histoire de l'Art pendant la Renaissance.* Vol. I. (Paris, 1889.)

Ozio. *Documenti diplomatici tratti degli Archivi Milanesi.* (Milano, 1864-72.)

Perrens. *Histoire de Florence.* (Paris, 1877-83.) *Histoire de Florence depuis la domination des Médicis jusqu'à la chute de la République.* (Paris, 1888.)

Poggio (Bracciolini). *Historiae Florentinae.* (In Vol. XX. of *Scriptt. rer. Italicarum*, ed. Muratori, Mediol., 1731.)

Rinuccini. *Ricordi storici dal 1282 al 1460.* (Firenze, 1840.)

Rio. *De l'Art Chrétien.* (Paris, 1861-67.)

Strozzi, Alessandro Macinghi negli. *Lettere d' una Gentildonna Fiorentina del secolo XV. ai figliuoli esuli.* (Pubbl. da C. Guasti, Firenze, 1877.)

Symonds. *The Renaissance in Italy.* (London, 1875-81.)

Vasari. *Le vite de' più eccellenti pittori, scultori, ed architetti.* (Ed. Milanesi, Firenze, 1878-85.)

Voigt. *Die Wiederlebung des classischen Alterthums.* (Berlin, 1859.)

Articles from the *Archivio Storico Italiano* (Firenze, 1842-96) and from the *Giornale Storico degli Archivi Toscani* (Firenze, 1857-63).

Foreign Statesmen

THE Publishers are issuing, under this title, the lives of eminent Statesmen of Continental Europe, corresponding in form and size, and similar in scope, to the series which, under the name "Twelve English Statesmen," was confined to the British Islands. The new Series does not aim at including every Statesman who has made his mark in the history of his country; it is necessarily limited to a selection from those who have exercised a commanding influence on the general course of European affairs, and impressed their memory deeply on the minds of men.

The Series is edited by Professor BURY, of Trinity College, Dublin. It includes, among others, the following:—

Charles the Great.
By THOMAS HODGKIN, D.C.L., Author of "Italy and Her Invaders," etc. [*Ready*.

Philip Augustus.
By Rev. W. H. HUTTON, Fellow and Tutor of St. John's College, Oxford. [*Ready*.

Louis XI.
By G. W. PROTHERO, Professor of History in the University of Edinburgh.

Charles the Fifth.
    By E. ARMSTRONG, Fellow of Queen's College Oxford.

William the Silent.
    By FREDERIC HARRISON. [*Ready.*

Philip the Second of Spain.
    By Colonel MARTIN HUME. [*Ready.*

Richelieu.
    By R. LODGE, Professor of History in the University of Glasgow. [*Ready.*

Mazarin.
    By ARTHUR H. HASSALL, Student and Tutor of Christ Church, Oxford.

Maria Theresa.
    By Dr. J. FRANCK BRIGHT, D.D., Master of University College, Oxford. [*Ready.*

Joseph II.
    By Dr. J. FRANCK BRIGHT, D.D. [*Ready.*

Catherine II.
    By J. B. BURY, Professor of Modern History in the University of Dublin.

Mirabeau.
    By P. F. WILLERT, Fellow of Exeter College, Oxford. [*Ready.*

Cavour.
    By the Countess MARTINENGO CESARESCO.

MACMILLAN AND CO., LTD., LONDON.

CPSIA information can be obtained at www.ICGtesting.com
Printed in the USA
BVOW09s0959210415
397042BV00012B/133/P